ADVANCES IN ACCOUNTING EDUCATION: TEACHING AND CURRICULUM INNOVATIONS

ADVANCES IN ACCOUNTING EDUCATION: TEACHING AND CURRICULUM INNOVATIONS

Series Editors: Timothy J. Rupert and Beth B. Kern

Recent Volumes:

ADVANCES IN ACCOUNTING EDUCATION: TEACHING
AND CURRICULUM INNOVATIONS
VOLUME 18

ADVANCES IN ACCOUNTING EDUCATION: TEACHING AND CURRICULUM INNOVATIONS

EDITED BY

TIMOTHY J. RUPERT
Northeastern University, USA

BETH B. KERN
Indiana University South Bend, USA

United Kingdom – North America – Japan
India – Malaysia – China

Emerald Group Publishing Limited
Howard House, Wagon Lane, Bingley BD16 1WA, UK

First edition 2016

British Library Cataloguing in Publication Data
A catalogue record for this book is available from the British Library

ISBN: 978-1-78560-767-7
ISSN: 1085-4622 (Series)

ISOQAR certified
Management System,
awarded to Emerald
for adherence to
Environmental
standard
ISO 14001:2004.

Certificate Number 1985
ISO 14001

INVESTOR IN PEOPLE

CONTENTS

LIST OF CONTRIBUTORS

Ira Abdullah	School of Business, Robert Morris University, Moon Township, PA, USA
Jason M. Bergner	College of Business, University of Nevada, Reno, Reno, NV, USA
Alisa G. Brink	School of Business, Virginia Commonwealth University, Richmond, VA, USA
William D. Brink	Farmer School of Business, Miami University, Oxford, OH, USA
Ann Boyd Davis	College of Business, Tennessee Tech University, Cookeville, TN, USA
C. Kevin Eller	Walker College of Business, Appalachian State University, Boone, NC, USA
Joshua J. Filzen	College of Business and Economics, Boise State University, Boise, ID, USA
Andrea Gouldman	School of Accounting & Taxation, Weber State University, Ogden, UT, USA
Ron Messer	School of Business, Kwantlen Polytechnic University, Surrey, British Columbia, Canada
Linda A. Quick	College of Business, East Carolina University, Greenville, NC, USA
Richard Rand	College of Business, Tennessee Tech University, Cookeville, TN, USA

Robert Seay   College of Business, Tennessee Tech
                       University, Cookeville, TN, USA

Jeffrey A. Wong   College of Business, University of Nevada,
                       Reno, Reno, NV, USA

Meifang Xiang   College of Business and Economics,
                       University of Wisconsin − Whitewater,
                       Whitewater, WI, USA

CALL FOR PAPERS

Submissions are invited for forthcoming volumes. *Advances in Accounting Education: Teaching and Curriculum Innovations* (AAETCI) publishes a wide variety of articles dealing with accounting education at the college and university level. AAETCI encourages readable, relevant, and reliable articles in all areas of accounting education including auditing, financial and managerial accounting, forensic accounting, governmental accounting, taxation, etc. Papers can be:

- Position papers on particular issues.
- Comprehensive literature reviews grounded in theory.
- Conceptual models.
- Historical discussions with implications for current and future pedagogical efforts.
- Methodology discussions.
- Pedagogical tools, including evidence of their effectiveness.
- Research studies with implications for improving accounting education.

AAETCI provides a forum for sharing generalizable teaching approaches from curricula development to content delivery techniques. Pedagogical research that contributes to more effective teaching in colleges and universities is highlighted. All articles must explain how teaching methods or curricula/programs can be improved. Non-empirical papers should be academically rigorous, and specifically discuss the institutional context of a course or program, as well as any relevant tradeoffs or policy issues. Empirical reports should exhibit sound research design and execution, and must develop a thorough motivation and literature review, possibly including references from outside the accounting field.

SUBMISSION PROCESS

Send two files by email: one with a manuscript copy but without a cover page, and the other solely a cover page with author information. Cover pages should list all authors' names and addresses (with telephone numbers, fax numbers, and e-mail addresses). The authors' names and addresses should not appear on the abstract. To assure anonymous review, authors should not identify themselves directly or indirectly. Also, attach a copy of any research instruments. Two reviewers assess each manuscript submitted and reviews are completed in a timely manner, usually 60–90 days.

Send manuscripts to aiae@neu.edu

WRITING GUIDELINES

1. Write your manuscript using active voice. Therefore, you can use the pronouns "we" and "I." Also, please avoid using a series of prepositional phrases. We strongly encourage you to use a grammar and spell checker on manuscripts before you submit to our journal. Parsimony is a highly desirable trait for manuscripts we publish. Be concise in making your points and arguments. The text of typical manuscripts (exclusive of references, tables, and appendices) are no longer than 30 pages.

2. Each paper should include a cover sheet with names, addresses, telephone numbers, fax numbers, and e-mail address for all authors. The title page also should include an abbreviated title that you should use as a running head (see item 7 below). The running head should be no more than 70 characters, which includes all letters, punctuation, and spaces between words.

3. The second page should consist of a Structured Abstract of no more than 250 words. Guidance for the Structured Abstract may be found at: http://www.emeraldgrouppublishing.com/authors/guides/write/abstracts.htm

    Abstracts from recent issues of *Advances in Accounting Education: Teaching and Curriculum Innovations* function as helpful examples.

4. You should begin the first page of the manuscript with the manuscript's title. DO NOT use the term "Introduction" or any other term at the beginning of the manuscript. Simply begin your discussion.

5. Use uniform margins of 1 1/2 inches at the top, bottom, right and left of every page. Do not justify lines, leave the right margins uneven. Do not hyphenate words at the end of a line; let a line run short or long rather than break a word. Type no more than 25 lines of text per page.

6. Double space all lines of text, which includes title, headings, and quotations.

7. All citations within your text should be formatted with the author(s) name and the year of publication. An appropriate citation is Catanach

(2004) or Catanach and Feldmann (2005), or Gaffney, Ryan, and Wurst (2010) when there are three or more authors. You do not need to cite six or seven references at once, particularly when the most recent references refer to earlier works. Please try to limit yourself to two or three citations at a time, preferably the most recent ones.

8. You should place page numbers for quotations along with the date of the material being cited. For example: According to Beaver (1987, 4), "Our knowledge of education research ... and its potential limitations for accounting ...."

9. Headings: Use headings and subheadings liberally to break up your text and ease the reader's ability to follow your arguments and train of thought.
   o First-level headings should be *UPPER CASE ITALICS*, bold face, and flush to the left margin.
     • Second level headings should be in *Bold Face Italics*, flush to the left margin with only the first letter of each primary word capitalized.
       • Third-level headings should be flush to the left margin, in *Italics* (but not bold face), with only the first letter of each primary word capitalized.

10. Notes or Endnotes should be used only if absolutely necessary. Try to incorporate endnote/footnote material into the body of the manuscript. Notes must be identified in the text by consecutive numbers, then enclosed in square brackets and listed at the end of the article. Place them on a separate section before your references. Begin notes on a separate page, with the word "Notes" centered at the top of the page. All notes should be double-spaced; indent the first line of each note five spaces.

11. Your reference pages should appear immediately after your "Notes" section (if any) and should include only works cited in the manuscript. The first page of this section should begin with the word "References" centered on the page. References to working papers are normally not appropriate. All references must be available to the reader; however, reference to unpublished dissertations is acceptable.

Sample Book References

Runkel, P. J., & McGrath, J. E. (1972). *Research on human behavior: A systematic guide to method.* New York, NY: Holt, Rinehart and Winston.

Smith, P. L. (1982). Measures of variance accounted for: Theory and practice. In Keren (Ed.), *Statistical and methodological issues in psychology and social science research* (pp. 101–129). Hillsdale, NJ: Erlbaum.

Sample Journal References

Abdolmohammadi, M. J., Menon, K., Oliver, T. W., & Umpathy, S. (1985). The role of the doctoral dissertation in accounting research careers. *Issues in Accounting Education, 22*, 59–76.

Thompson, B. (1993). The use of statistical significance tests in research: Bootstrap and other methods. *Journal of Experimental Education, 61*, 361–377.

Simon, H. A. (1980). The behavioral and social sciences. *Sciences*, (July), 72–78.

Electronic Sources

If available online, the full URL should be supplied at the end of the reference.

American Institute of Certified Public Accountants (AICPA). (1999). *Core competency framework for the accounting profession.* Retrieved from http://www.aicpa.org/edu/corecomp.htm

12. You should label TABLES and FIGURES as such and number them consecutively (using Arabic numerals) in the order in which you mention them first in the text. Indicate the approximate placement of each table/figure by a clear break in the text, inserting:

    TABLE (or FIGURE) 1 ABOUT HERE

    Figures should be placed after your References section and tables should follow figures. Begin each table and figure on a separate page.
13. You should list any acknowledgments on a separate page in a separate electronic file to preserve author anonymity. Type the word

"Acknowledgment," centered, at the top of the page and type the acknowledgment itself as a double-spaced, single paragraph. Once the editorial review process is complete, your acknowledgments will be inserted immediately after the last page of text (before the Notes and References Sections).

14. The proper order for sections of your manuscript should be: title page, structured abstract, main text, acknowledgements (once editorial process is complete), appendix, references, figures and finally tables.

15. After you have arranged the manuscript pages in correct order, number them consecutively, beginning with the title page. Number all pages. Place the number in the upper right-hand corner using Arabic numerals. Identify each manuscript page by typing an abbreviated title (header) above the page number.

EDITORIAL REVIEW BOARD

STATEMENT OF PURPOSE

Advances in Accounting Education: Teaching and Curriculum Innovations is a refereed academic journal whose purpose is to meet the needs of individuals interested in the educational process. We publish thoughtful, well-developed articles that are readable, relevant, and reliable.

Articles may be non-empirical or empirical. Our emphasis is pedagogy, and articles MUST explain how instructors can improve teaching methods or accounting units can improve curricula/programs.

Non-empirical manuscripts should be academically rigorous. They can be theoretical syntheses, conceptual models, position papers, discussions of methodology, comprehensive literature reviews grounded in theory, or historical discussions with implications for current and future efforts. Reasonable assumptions and logical development are essential. All manuscripts should discuss implications for research and/or teaching.

Sound research design and execution are critical for empirical reports. All articles should have well-articulated and strong theoretical foundations, and establishing a link to the non-accounting literature is desirable.

REVIEW PROCEDURES

Advances in Accounting Education: Teaching and Curriculum Innovations will provide authors with timely reports that clearly indicate the review status of the manuscript. Authors will receive the results of initial reviews normally within eight to twelve weeks of manuscript submission, if not earlier. We expect authors to work with a co-editor who will act as a liaison between the authors and the reviewers to resolve areas of concern.

IMPROVING THE QUALITY OF LEARNING IN ACCOUNTING THROUGH ADVICE AND LEARNING EXPERIENCES FROM FORMER STUDENTS [☆]

Meifang Xiang

ABSTRACT

Purpose — *The primary purpose of this study is to introduce a method of using former students' advice and learning experiences to affect subsequent students' thoughts and beliefs about accounting learning in a positive way thereby improving their academic performance.*

Methodology/approach — *At the end of Fall 2009, the instructor invited the students to give suggestions to future accounting students about their learning experiences. On the first days of the following three semesters, I showed the feedback to the subsequent students. I recommended that the students read the suggestions after class and throughout the semester when necessary. I also conduct the survey to collect the students'*

[☆]Data Availability: Data is available upon request. Please contact the author.

Advances in Accounting Education: Teaching and Curriculum Innovations, Volume 18, 1–22
ISSN: 1085-4622/doi:10.1108/S1085-462220160000018001

perceptions on the usefulness of former students' advice. Analyses are conducted to assess the impact of the students' advice on class attendance, exam performance, and the dropout rate for the course.

Findings – *The results show that former students' advice and learning experiences can help subsequent students improve class attendance, course performance, and the drop rate.*

Social implications – *The study provides a useful and easy-to-adopt learning supplement to help students succeed in a course that many students find challenging. The study also gives educators a simple but useful and efficient way to achieve greater student involvement in their learning processes.*

Originality/value – *To the best of my knowledge, this study is the first to focus on the impact of former students' advice and learning experience on the following students' learning performance in accounting education.*

Keywords: Former students' advice; peer feedback; peer assessment; social-psychological interventions in education; academic performance

Tough (2014) indicates that many college freshmen experience academic setbacks or face hard times during the first semester/year in college. The students tend to take difficulties seriously and believe that they will be permanent instead temporary. Therefore, the student may be depressed believing that he/she does not belong in college which can contribute to a high dropout rate. This phenomenon is also true for accounting education, especially for the first accounting course. Phillips and Schmidt (2010) state that students generally have difficulty in comprehending topics such as accrual accounting, journal entries, and adjusting entries, all of which are covered in the first college-level financial accounting course. Therefore, it is no surprise that students generally rank the course as the most challenging first-year or second-year course, characterizing it as both difficult and time-consuming (Bergin, 1983; Xiang & Gruber, 2012).

There are a couple of reasons for the phenomenon. First, accounting itself is a complex and challenging field. The complexities of the profession and practice have been increasing as economic conditions around the world are increasing in complexity (Fellingham, 2007; Turner, 2006). Second, new accounting students tend to be too optimistic about the entry-level accounting course. For example, one survey I conducted during the first days of the four semesters (between 2009 and 2011) showed that most students expected a final grade of an A or B. They did not know that only about half of the students achieve grades of B or above, while the other half earn grades of C or below and some fail the course. Another survey (focusing on students repeating the course) I conducted showed that the main reasons given for having to retake the course were: did not take the course seriously, did not work hard enough, and/or thought the course was easy.

Unfortunately, accounting instructors can do little to change the fact that accounting is a challenging course. Fortunately, accounting professors can do something to help students prepare for the challenge as early as possible. As Yeager and Walton (2011) explain in their study on the positive effect of social-psychological interventions, educators can improve learning by targeting students' feelings, thoughts, and beliefs instead of teaching extra academic content.

The main purpose of this study is to introduce one method of using advice and learning experiences from former students (former students' advice hereafter) to affect subsequent students' thoughts and beliefs about accounting learning in a positive way, therefore improving their academic performance. This study provides evidence of the usefulness of using former students' advice in the hope that it will convince accounting instructors, especially instructors of the entry-level accounting courses, to seriously consider adopting a similar approach.

One main difference between this study and preceding studies is that most prior research investigates students who are mentoring or providing advice contemporaneously with the students taking the course. In this study, prior and subsequent students do not meet each other. Topping (1998, p. 254) called it "no face-to-face contact." Based on a review of the literature, this is the first study in accounting to focus on taking advantage of social-psychological intervention to help students identify the challenges, their strengths and weaknesses, target areas for remedial action, avoid overestimation or underestimation, and to improve academic performance and/or maximize success.

The remainder of the chapter is organized as follows. The next section reviews the background information on peer-assisted learning and feedback as well as the role of social-psychological interventions in education. The hypotheses follow this section. The methodology section discusses the sample used, the intervention adopted, and the models used to test hypotheses. A discussion of the results and their implications concludes the chapter.

BACKGROUND

Two streams of literature are relevant to this study. The first focuses on peer-assisted learning and peer feedback. The second concerns social-psychological interventions in education.

Peer-Assisted Learning and Peer Feedback

Boud, Cohen, and Sampson (1999) define peers as people with similar experience or in similar situations (not teachers or experts) who share the status of fellow learners and are accepted by each other. Peer-assisted learning can take various forms. Examples include self-help groups, senior students' groups that mentor junior groups, and student-organized supplemental-study groups. Many institutions of higher education around the world have adopted peer-assisted learning approaches. Examples include, Supplemental Instruction (SI) in America (Congos & Schoeps, 1993), Peer-Assisted Student Support (PASS) in the United Kingdom (Atkins, May, & Marks-Maran, 2005; Packham & Miller, 2000), and Peer-Assisted Learning (PAL) in Australia (Dobbie & Joyce, 2008; Jackling & McDowall, 2008). The past few years have seen an abundance of research on peer-assisted learning as a useful mechanism for improving students' academic performance (see, Adler & Milne, 1997; Cottell & Millis, 1992; Falchikov & Blythman, 2001; Topping, 1996, 2005). In fact, many researchers and educators consider peer-assisted learning to be an efficient method for improving learning quality (Boud & Lee, 2005; Ginsburg-Block, Rohrbeck, & Fantuzzo, 2006). Several previous studies show that students learn a lot by explaining their thoughts to others and by participating in activities in which they can learn from other students (Candy, Crebert, & O'leary, 1994; Farrell & Farrell, 2008).

Vygotsky (1980) was one of the first to research peer assessment. He presented the concept of scaffolded learning: internal thoughts from one group can lead or encourage the other group to follow and to interact, especially when the assessors can provide feedback on both weaknesses and strengths, and provide suggestions. Van Lehn, Chi, Baggett, and Murray (1995) provided evidence that peer assessment, one format of which is peer feedback, in general, can help peers to reinforce and have better and deeper self-understanding.

Falchikov (1995) designed an experiment to study the impact of peer feedback. The results showed that peer feedback has a positive effect with helping students improve the quality of learning, having a better sense of accountability and responsibility thereby developing appropriate metacognition. Topping's (1998) review of peer assessment and peer feedback indicates that with the help of a prior group's experience and performance, the following group can make more accurate self-assessments, plan their own learning process, target problems or errors, and enhance engagement. Similar extant studies also show that peer feedback is associated with better quality thinking, more accurate self-assessment and identity, and fewer repetitive mistakes (Bangert-Drowns, Kulik, Kulik, & Morgan, 1991; Kulik & Kulik, 1988).

Social-Psychological Interventions in Education

The current study intends to provide evidence that prior students' advice can help subsequent students change their thoughts, beliefs, and attitudes and therefore increase their performance in the first accounting course. Several researchers have examined this issue. Wilson and Linville (1982, 1985) designed a study to examine the differences between two groups. One group watched a video in which older students shared their experiences and struggles during their early years of college and how they managed to improve, while the control group did not. The results showed that the academic performance of the group with peer guidance reported an improved GPA in later years. However, the group not exposed to peer guidance did not have an improved GPA. Following Wilson and Linville (1982, 1985), Good, Aronson, and Inzlicht (2003) studied seventh grade students and provided evidence that female students improve their test performance in math over a control group when receiving mentoring from college students. The results also showed that minority and low-income students receiving mentoring reported improved test performance in reading over a control group. Blackwell, Trzesniewski, and Dweck (2007) also examined seventh grade students and provided similar evidence that mentorship from college students is associated with more positive attitudes and therefore better class performance over that of a control group.

Yeager and Walton (2011) reviewed social-psychological interventions such as brief and small exercises focusing on changing students' thoughts and beliefs and concluded that those interventions can improve student's academic performance. They believe that social-psychological interventions, if coordinated well with other reforms and methods, can solve many challenges in education related to learning performance. Yeager and Walton also initiated interventions for struggling students at the University of Texas-Austin and community-colleges. Their goal was to help the struggling students by changing their beliefs about their abilities and sense of belonging with a simple intervention which took only 25−45 minutes. Their studies show that the students' stress levels were reduced, as were their negative thoughts about their abilities. Academic performance improved with the dropout rate decreasing from 20% to 9% in one community college. From a psychological point of view, Yeager and Walton's study provides a theoretical basis for many prior peer-assisted learning studies.

HYPOTHESES

Many extant studies have shown that peer-assisted learning and peer feedback have a positive relationship with more active engagement, more efficient time use, more self-confidence, earlier identification of errors or misconceptions, and better course performance as a whole (Boud, 1990; Crooks, 1988; Falchikov, 1995; Mowl & Pain, 1995; Richer, 1992). Based on prior research (e.g., Doran & Bouillon, 1991; Schroeder, 1986; Topping, 1998; Xiang & Gruber, 2012; Yeager & Walton, 2011), the current study intends to investigate whether former students' advice has any impact on subsequent students. Specifically, the following three hypotheses are investigated:

H1. Students provided with former students' advice attend class more regularly than students who are not.

H2. Students provided with former students' advice achieve higher exam scores than students who are not.

H3. Students provided with former students' advice are less likely to drop the course than students who are not.

METHODOLOGY

Sample and Participants

The university used in the current study is located in the Midwest of the United States and is known for its high quality, career-oriented undergraduate and graduate programs. The university is accredited by the North Central Association of Colleges and Universities and its college of business is accredited by the Association to Advance Collegiate Schools of Business (AACSB).

Introduction to Financial Accounting is a required course for all business majors and it is the first accounting course in the business curriculum. Class size is generally limited to 40–50 students. Total enrollment, including all sections of the course, is typically between 600 and 650 students in the fall semester and between 200 and 250 students in the spring semester. Student learning is assessed using three mid-term exams, one final exam, five projects, and other assignments (e.g., homework) throughout the semester. Four exams primarily determine approximately 79% of a student's final grade with the projects and other assignments about 11% and 10%, respectively. One experienced instructor (the "course coordinator") is responsible for developing the exams and projects as well as coordinating the four to eight instructors who teach the course each semester. The coordinator is also responsible for maintaining the quality and consistency of the course throughout the years.

This study uses data from 15 sections taught by a single instructor (the author of the current study) over a five-semester period (three sections in each of the following semesters: Spring 2009, Fall 2009, Spring 2010, Fall 2010, and Fall 2011).[1] In the first two semesters (Spring 2009 and Fall 2009, *SEMESTERS WITHOUT ADVICE* hereafter), the students did not receive former students' advice. A total of 270 students were registered for the six sections in these two semesters. The study eliminated 7 students who were retaking the course and 24 students who dropped the course, yielding 239 students who formed the control group. In the following three semesters (Spring 2010, Fall 2010, and Fall 2011, *SEMESTERS WITH ADVICE* hereafter), the students received former students' advice. A little over 400 students (406 in total) were registered for the next three semesters. The study eliminated 21 students who were retaking the course and 14 students dropped the course, yielding 371 students who formed the experimental group. Therefore, about a total of 610 students comprised the total sample. Although the use of a single instructor may affect the generalizability of this study's results, it controls for potential bias caused by the differences in the teaching styles of the various instructors.

Intervention

At the end of Fall 2009, the instructor invited the students to give suggestions (in a format of a few sentences, a short paragraph, or a short essay) to future accounting students, about their learning experiences. Though not required to do so, the students were enthusiastic in sharing their suggestions and learning experiences. About 70% of the students provided suggestions and experiences to subsequent students.

In general, the former students offered the subsequent students detailed information on how to succeed in the entry-level accounting course. They focused on their general opinions about the course, their experiences, their suggestions, and the tips on how to learn the course topics. They provided suggestions on the importance of regular class attendance, active assignments practice, engaged textbook reading, studying for the exam, not slacking off after the first mid-term, and staying focused during the whole semester. For example, a typical suggestion and comment is: *"When you are told at the beginning of this semester that you will need to read the chapters, come to class and practice homework more than once, they are not kidding. Falling behind is very easy to do if you slack."* In other words, the students' suggestions cover a large portion, if not all of the key elements of success that an instructor would like to emphasize for new accounting students (see Table 1 for more details).

After getting the students' submissions in Fall 2009, the instructor saved all of the students feedback.[2] On the first days of the three *SEMESTERS WITH ADVICE*, the instructor showed PowerPoint slides summarizing feedback for the new students. After the first day of class, the instructor posted the PowerPoint slides and the PDF file (with all Fall 2009 students' advice and experiences included) on the campus Intranet. The instructor recommended that the students read the suggestions after class and throughout the semester when necessary, especially after the first mid-term exam, when students had some idea of the content of the accounting course. In addition, the instructor encouraged the students to reread the suggestions and to check the methods they had used during the past few weeks after each exam to see whether there was any room for improvement.

Instrument and Data Collection

Prior studies have provided a variety of assessment methods for demonstrating that students can learn more effectively via new strategies or innovations (see Burns, 2006; Melé, 2005, for a review). The current study assesses the impact of former students' advice via both qualitative and quantitative measures using a similar method to that of Lavoie and Rosman (2007), Hurtt and Thomas (2008), and Massey and Van Hise (2009). Similar to Blackwell et al. (2007), surveys were given to students collecting information concerning: (1) students' learning attitude changes pre- versus post-receiving former students' advice; and (2) comments on the usefulness of former students' advice. In the comments, students were

Table 1.   Types of Former Students' Advice and Learning Experiences.

Types of Feedback	Students' Advice
General advice about the course	• "As a student who had never had an accounting course, **the key to success in this course is determination**. Is it a lot of work? Yes. Is it difficult? Yes. Is it impossible? No …" • **"This class is as hard as everyone else says it is.** There is no joke when people say that it's the hardest class they've taken." • "READ! There is no way someone can be successful in this course if you don't read each chapter AT LEAST once. You **really need to work hard from the 'get-go' in this class** or you'll find yourself in a hole that's not fun to get out of!"
Class attendance	• **"I made the mistake of never showing up to class and I had to study hard to try and keep up with the class.** The most important thing I can recommend is to go to class each day and keep up with the work." • "I would suggest that you really read the chapter and do all of the (online) quizzes, it also really helps and is important that you do all of the homework and projects, it helps one understand the material and **NEVER MISS CLASS!!!!**" • "My suggestion for future students is to read the chapters before you go to class. It will help you understand the material better. Also, **do not skip any classes.** You should do all your homework and projects. After the lecture, you should go to any SI sessions available. Before the tests re-read the chapters and then look over all the hand-outs, notes, homework and projects."
Exams and learning performance	• "Don't wait till last minute! I wish I could go back and take more time to understand the information. **Study for the test and take this course very seriously!!**" • "If you took an accounting course before the first test will probably be easy for you but after that one they get much harder. **DO NOT SLACK AFTER THE FIRST TEST!!!!!!!!!!!!**" • "In order to be successful, there are many things to do. **If you want to get an A in this course, you are going to need to do a lot of work** … If you do all these suggestions, you should be able to do fine in the class."
Other advice	• "… **Go ask the professor if you are not clear on something.** I did not do that and really regret not taking advantage of the professor's knowledge, so I really encourage other students to not make my mistake and ASK!" • "**Read the chapters more than once.** Read the chapters before coming to class. **PRACTICE, PRACTICE, PRACTICE!!!**" • "The best advice I can offer to incoming students is to **TAKE THE PROFESSOR'S ADVICE!!!**

asked to explain their answers. Similar to prior research (Doran & Bouillon, 1991; Gist, Goedde, & Ward, 1996; Gracia, & Jenkins, 2002), students' class attendance, exam performance, and the dropout rate are tested using both univariate and multivariate analysis.

Models Used

Extant studies have shown that many factors potentially have an impact on students' academic and course performance. For example, students' former study experiences have a positive impact on student course performance (Baldwin & Howe, 1982; Geiger & Ogilby, 2000; Hartnett, Romcke, & Yap, 2004; Hellstén, 2004; Rankin, Silvester, Vallely, & Wyatt, 2003). Doran and Bouillon (1991) show that GPA, SAT, and former accounting course(s) are important in explaining student academic performance in the first university-level accounting course. They also provided evidence that gender is associated with student performance. Xiang and Gruber (2012) examine the impact of former high school accounting education on the first college-level accounting course using a model including factors such as gender, major, year in school, class attendance, and assignments performance. The results show that there is a positive and significant relationship between prior accounting education in high school and the course performance in the first post-secondary accounting course. In other words, students with prior accounting education are more likely to pass this course successfully. Their results also need to be interpreted carefully. For example, prior accounting education does not guarantee superlative grades.

To test H1, consistent with Xiang and Gruber (2012), Ordinary Least Square regression (OLS) is employed to assess students' attendance. The regression model for students' attendance is:

$$
\begin{aligned}
Attendance_i = \alpha + {} & \beta_1 Gender_i + \beta_2 Year\_In\_School_i + \beta_3 GPA_i \\
& + \beta_4 With\_High\_School\_Accounting\_Course_i \qquad (1) \\
& + \beta_5 With\_Former\_Students'\_Advice_i + \varepsilon
\end{aligned}
$$

where the dependent variable, *Attendance*, is a continuous variable based upon the number of absences the student had during that semester. The independent variables are *Gender*, *Year_in_School*, *GPA*, *With_High_School_Accounting_Course*, and *With_Former_Students'_Advice*. Specifically, *Gender* is a dummy variable taking the value one if male, and zero otherwise. *Year_in_School* takes the value of 1−5 (1, freshman; 2, sophomore; 3, junior; 4, senior; and 5, graduate). *GPA* refers to the cumulative college grade-point-average (4.0 scale) information when taking the first university-level accounting course. The variable *With_Former_Students'_Advice* is a dummy variable taking the value one if the student received former students' advice, and zero otherwise.

To test H2, OLS regression is employed to examine students' exam performance. The regression model for the examine performance takes the following form:

$$Exam\_Score_i = \alpha + \beta_1 Gender_i + \beta_2 Year\_In\_School_i + \beta_3 GPA_i$$
$$+ \ \beta_4 With\_High\_School\_Accounting\_Course_i \qquad (2)$$
$$+ \ \beta_5 With\_Former\_Students'\_Advice_i + \varepsilon_i$$

where the dependent variable, *Exam_Score*, is a continuous variable based upon student's total exam score in points in the course.

To test H3, logistic regression is used to examine students' dropping out. The regression model for students' dropping out is:

$$Drop\_the\_Course_i = \alpha + \beta_1 Gender_i + \beta_2 Year\_In\_School_i + \beta_3 GPA_i$$
$$+ \ \beta_4 With\_High\_School\_Accounting\_Course_i \qquad (3)$$
$$+ \ \beta_5 With\_Former\_Students'\_Advice_i + \varepsilon_i$$

where the dependent variable, *Drop_the_Course*, is a dummy variable taking the value one if the student dropped the course one week before the first exam or thereafter, and zero otherwise.

RESULTS

Survey Results

In Fall 2010 two similar surveys were administered to the students receiving peer advice (132 in total) on the first day of the semester. One survey was given before they received any advice from former students while the other was given to the same group of students after they got the former students' advice.

The first survey included questions that asked their opinions about the importance of (1) taking the course seriously, (2) going to class regularly, (3) reading the textbook, (4) practicing homework, and (5) practicing sample exams. The importance of each item was ranked from 1 to 7, with one representing a level of not important at all to seven representing a level of very important. The first survey also asked the students their expected grade in the course. After they submitted the first survey, the students were provided with former students' advice. Finally, at the end of the first day of class, the same students were invited to complete the second survey, which was very similar to the first one.

Table 2 shows the responses to the survey at the beginning and end of the first day of Fall 2010. A comparison of respondents' perceptions at the beginning and ending of the day reveals statistically significant changes with respect to increased importance of (1) taking the course seriously ($p < 0.05$); (2) going to class regularly ($p < 0.05$); (3) reading the textbook ($p < 0.05$); and (4) practicing homework ($p < 0.10$). In addition the students lowered their grade expectation from an A or B to a B. For example, before receiving suggestions from former students, more than half of the students were expecting a grade of A, whereas the percentage decreased to 39% after receiving former students' advice. Similarly, in the first survey, only 1.5% students replied that they expected a grade of C, whereas in the second survey, the number increased to nearly 10%. Although students remained overly optimistic regarding their potential

Table 2. Shifting of Following Students' Attitude before/after Receiving Former Students' Advice (Paired Samples) ($n = 113$).[a]

Survey Questions	Mean Pre-Former Students' Advice	Mean Post-Former Students' Advice	t-Test[b]
Please rank from 1 (not important at all) to 7 (very important)			
What is your opinion on the importance of the following items in learning the first college-level accounting course?			
Taking the course seriously	6.53	6.69	−2.01**
Going to class regularly	6.68	6.85	−2.10**
Reading the textbook	5.81	6.19	−2.73**
Practicing homework	6.18	6.54	−1.55*
Practicing sample exams	6.55	6.62	−0.72
What is your expected grade? (A, B, C, D, or F)	A/B	B	−5.91***

[a]19 surveys are deleted for missing information.
[b]Differences are significant at *$p < 0.10$, **$p < 0.05$, and ***$p < 0.001$.

grade, at least their expectations were closer to the reality of the challenges they would face.

At the end of the *SEMESTERS WITH ADVICE*, the students involved in the study were invited to complete a survey about their opinions of their former students' advice: "What is your opinion about the impact of the suggestions from former students, given on the first day of the semester?," with a scale from 1 to 7 (one representing "totally useless" and seven representing "very useful"). A total of 294 out of 334 students (88%) stated that the suggestions were useful (rated 5 or above). Students were also asked to write a detailed explanation of their answers. Table 3 shows some typical comments from the students during *SEMESTERS WITH ADVICE*. Based on the comments, the majority of students receiving peer advice gave comments that the former students' guidance is very useful.

The survey results provide some evidence that peer advice is associated with a shift in students' attitudes regarding behaviors that can potentially lead to enhanced learning. The surveys also indicate that the students found peer advice useful. But, do these shifts in attitudes lead to changes in behavior and enhanced student learning outcomes?

Table 3.   Typical Students' Comments after Using Former Students' Advice.

- "All of the suggestions showed in class were very helpful and very accurate. They gave the new students an idea about how hard this class really is."
- "This first day of class is the most important day of the semester because the advice you get will help lay the foundation for your success in this class."
- "Taking the advice was the smartest thing I believe I have done this year for this class. If I didn't put so much effort into this class, I surely would've failed."
- "The student suggestions were helpful because it told us what to expect and how to prepare for the class."
- "The first day I was scared, but I'm happy I was scared. Otherwise, I don't think I would have done as well as I did."
- "I would not have read all the chapters and done the homework without the sincere warnings. It was good advice."
- "I chose not to follow the advice given and slacked. I have been behind all semester. This class you actually have to read the book."
- "If I would have followed the suggestions given, I probably would have done better in the class."
- "After the first test I did become a little lazy and the second test hit me hard. I should have listened more to the persistence parts."

Class Attendance Results

H1 examines if peer advice is associated with changes in student behavior, specifically attendance. In all *SEMESTERS WITH ADVICE*, students generally had better class attendance than *SEMESTERS WITHOUT ADVICE* (see Table 4). Specifically, the mean absence rates for *SEMESTERS WITH ADVICE* were 2.21 days, 1.58 days, and 1.57 days, respectively, compared with 4.22 days and 2.94 days for *SEMESTERS WITHOUT ADVICE*. Results show that the difference of class absences between the semesters with or without former students' advice is significant ($p < 0.01$).

The regression results presented in column 1 of Table 5 provide further analyses of the relationship between whether or not a student received former students' advice and the number of his or her absences during the semester. The results show students who received advice from former students missed fewer classes than those who did not, and this difference is statistically significant ($p < 0.01$). Therefore, there is evidence of an association between peer advice and improved attendance after controlling for gender, year in school, GPA, and having taken a prior high school accounting course.

Course Performance Results

H2 attempts to assess if there is evidence of a relationship between peer advice and improved student learning outcomes in the form of better exam scores. Students who received peer advice received an average exam score of 71.5% versus an exam score of 68.6% for students who did not receive peer advice. The difference is statically significant ($p < 0.05$).

Column 2 of Table 5 presents the outcome of analyzing exam scores controlling for other factors which can affect a student's exam performance. The results show that former students' advice has a statically significant positive effect on subsequent students' performance ($p < 0.01$). Specifically, students receiving former students' advice tend to achieve higher exam scores than students not receiving former students' advice. Table 5 also shows that students with higher cumulative GPA ($p < 0.01$) and students who have some high school accounting ($p < 0.01$) tend to earn higher exam scores than other students, which is consistent with Doran and Bouillon (1991), Gist et al. (1996), and Xiang and Gruber (2012).

Table 4. Summary Statistics of Class Absences.

Information of Absences	Semester without Former Students' Advice		Semester with Former Students' Advice			Absences Comparison		
	Spring 2009	Fall 2009	Spring 2010	Fall 2010	Fall 2011	Mean of semesters without former students' advice	Mean of semesters with former students' advice	t-Test
Mean absences	4.22	2.94	2.21	1.58	1.57	3.49	1.78	4.77***
Students with no absences	31.73%	31.85%	53.28%	49.61%	59.01%			
Students with 2 or fewer absences	61.53%	70.37%	75.41%	78.74%	83.61%			
Students with 4–9 absences	17.31%	15.55%	9.83%	10.24%	5.74%			
Students with 10 or more absences	10.71%	8.14%	8.20%	0.78%	4.92%			
Total number of students	104	135	122	127	122			

Table 5. Relationship between Former Students' Advice and Attendance,
Total Exam Score, and Probability of Dropping Out.

	Attendance (1)	Total Exam Score (2)	Dropout (3)
Intercept	47.912	9.911	1.374
	(21.015)**	(1.618)***	(1.146)**
Gender	7.490	1.077	−0.102
	(4.775)	(0.367)**	(0.367)
Year in school	−1.059	−0.002	0.006
	(5.335)	(0.410)	(0.345)
GPA	62.470	−2.162	−1.030
	(4.789)***	(0.368)***	(0.222)***
High school accounting course	30.232	−0.614	−1.411
	(4.830)***	(0.371)*	(0.457)***
Former students' advice	14.992	−1.818	−1.255
	(4.865)***	(0.374)***	(0.372)***
Adj. R^2 (Pseudo-R^2 for logistic regression)	30.33%	11.77%	18.23%
Observations	558	558	596

Notes: The table reports the results from Ordinary Least Square (OLS) regression for columns (1) and (2). Logistic regression is used for column (3).
The dependent variables are (1) Attendance measured by the number of absences during a semester, (2) total exam score is the total exam points for the semester, and (3) dropout is a dichotomous variable with a value of one if the student dropped the course one week before the first exam or thereafter, and zero otherwise.
*, **, ***Statistically significant at the 0.10, 0.05, and 0.01 levels, respectively.

Because exams vary from semester to semester, exam performance in the sections receiving peer advice is compared to contemporaneous sections not receiving peer advice but having the same exam. I taught the experimental sections; other instructors taught the sections without peer advice. Because instructors can influence learning, comparisons in exam performance are provided both prior to and during the semesters with intervention.

The left portion of Table 6 compares exam scores for sections I taught versus those by other instructors. None of these sections had the experimental intervention of peer advice. The results show that in the semesters in which neither I nor the other instructors had a peer advice intervention the average exam scores of each semester were around the same level with those of the other sections. However, after students were given the former students' advice, the average exam scores for the students who received peer advice were much higher (2−4%, about 13−18 points or 6−9 more

Table 6. Comparison of Average Exam Points between Tested Sections and Sections Taught by Other Instructors.

Semesters	Semester without Former Students' Advice				Semester with Former Students' Advice					
	Spring 2009		Fall 2009		Spring 2010		Fall 2010		Fall 2011	
Sections	Test instructor sections	Other sections	Test instructor sections	Other sections	Experimental instructor sections	Other sections	Experimental instructor sections	Other sections	Experimental instructor sections	Other sections
Exam score	65.96%	67.35%	70.63%	72.66%	67.66%	63.65%	75.53%	70.92%	71.20%	67.82%
Number of students	104	96	135	466	122	101	127	479	122	488

correct answers out of 44 questions) than those of other sections.[3] These results provide additional evidence of an association between peer advice and improved learning outcomes in the form of exam scores thereby supporting H2.

Student Dropout Rate Results

H3 tests students' dropout rates to ascertain whether students receiving former students' advice were less likely to withdraw from the course. The dropout rates in every section with peer advice were lower than the dropout rates before the peer guidance intervention was introduced. For example, prior to the peer advice intervention, the dropout rate was 8.40% and 9.27% in each semester. Once the peer advice intervention was introduced the dropout rate decreased to 5.56%, 0.76% and 3.84%, respectively, for each semester. The difference in the dropout rate between the semesters with and without former students' advice is significant ($p < 0.01$).

Column 3 of Table 5 presents the results of the logistic regression related to the probability of dropping the course. The results show that adopting former students' advice decreased the probability of a student dropping the course and the effect is significant at the 1% level. Therefore, H3 is supported.

In sum, the above analyses show an association between peer advice and improved class attendance, better exam performance and a lower likelihood of dropping a course.

DISCUSSION AND CONCLUSIONS

The current study contributes to the accounting education literature in at least two ways. First, this study provides a useful and easy-to-adopt learning supplement to help students succeed in a course that many students find challenging. Second, it gives educators a simple but useful and efficient way to achieve greater student involvement in their learning processes. Just as Yeager and Walton (2011) presented in their study: instead of teaching additional academic content, social-psychological interventions (which focus on having a positive effect on students' thoughts and beliefs) can increase students' academic performance in a noticeable way.

There are some limitations of the study. First, some efforts were made to reduce the possibility of other factors affecting the results (e.g., the first semester in which the specific instructor taught the course was excluded). However, it is possible that other factors, which are not measured in this study such as student experiences from other classes, family factors, related work experience, and cultural differences, may have impact on students' motivation in learning accounting. Unfortunately, the current study does not have available data to examine these factors. Second, the current study has been limited to a comparatively small number of students at one mid-western institution. Future research should evaluate whether the approach suggested is also robust for other accounting courses (e.g., intermediate accounting, managerial accounting, tax and auditing), at other universities, or for universities in other countries. Third, the data collected in this study are joint tests of all the students' advice. Therefore, it is difficult to ascertain the effects of specific types of feedback on student performance. Thus, the current study only scratches the surface of peer advice. Future avenues for research include improving self-motivation and the duration of the effects of peer guidance.

NOTES

1. The first semester that the instructor taught this course was not included in the study to remove the potential bias caused by changes in the teaching style or method.
2. This is not provided because of the length of the file. It is available if requested.
3. More statistical analyses (the relationship between former students' advice and students' performance on course assignments, and the relationship between former students' advice and the performance of the whole semester (including both exams and assignments)) are also tested. The results are consistent with the basic regression analysis reported in Table 5. Those regression analyses are not reported here for brevity. They are available if requested.

ACKNOWLEDGMENT

The author would like to thank two anonymous referees and Beth B. Kern (editor) for helpful comments leading to a significant improvement in the content and exposition of the chapter. The author also thanks the conference participants at the Global Business and Social Science Research Conference, and Linda Holmes, for their comments and suggestions.

REFERENCES

Adler, R. W., & Milne, M. J. (1997). Improving the quality of accounting students' learning through action-oriented learning tasks. *Journal of Accounting Education, 6*(3), 191–215.

Atkins, N., May, S., & Marks-Maran, D. (2005). Widening participation in subjects requiring data handling skills: The MathsAid Project. *Journal of Further and Higher Education, 29*(4), 353–365.

Baldwin, B. A., & Howe, K. R. (1982). Secondary-level study of accounting and subsequent performance in the first college course. *The Accounting Review, 57*(3), 619–626.

Bangert-Drowns, R. L., Kulik, C. L. C., Kulik, J. A., & Morgan, M. (1991). The instructional effect of feedback in test-like events. *Review of Educational Research, 61*(2), 213–238.

Bergin, J. L. (1983). The effect of previous accounting study on student performance in the first college-level financial accounting course. *Issues in Accounting Education, 1*, 19–28.

Blackwell, L. S., Trzesniewski, K. H., & Dweck, C. S. (2007). Implicit theories of intelligence predict achievement across an adolescent transition: A longitudinal study and an intervention. *Child Development, 78*(1), 246–263.

Boud, D. (1990). Assessment and the promotion of academic values. *Studies in Higher Education, 15*(1), 101–111.

Boud, D., Cohen, R., & Sampson, J. (1999). Peer learning and assessment. *Assessment and Evaluation in Higher Education, 24*(4), 413–426.

Boud, D., & Lee, A. (2005). 'Peer learning' as pedagogic discourse for research education. *Studies in Higher Education, 30*(5), 501–516.

Burns, C. S. (2006). The evolution of a graduate capstone accounting course. *Journal of Accounting Education, 24*(2–3), 118–133.

Candy, P. C., Crebert, G., & O'leary, J. (1994). *Developing lifelong learners through undergraduate education.* Canberra: Australian Government Publishing Service.

Congos, D. H., & Schoeps, N. (1993). Does supplemental instruction really work and what is it anyway? *Studies in Higher Education, 18*(2), 165–176.

Cottell, P. G., & Millis, B. J. (1992). Cooperative learning in accounting. *Journal of Accounting Education, 10*(1), 95–111.

Crooks, T. J. (1988). The impact of classroom evaluation practices on students. *Review of Educational Research, 58*(4), 438–481.

Dobbie, M., & Joyce, S. (2008). Peer-assisted learning in accounting: A qualitative assessment. *Asian Social Science, 4*(3), 18–25.

Doran, B. M., & Bouillon, M. L. (1991). Determinants of student performance in accounting principles I and II. *Issues in Accounting Education, 6*(1), 74–84.

Falchikov, N. (1995). Peer feedback marking: Developing peer assessment. *Programmed Learning, 32*(2), 175–187.

Falchikov, N., & Blythman, M. (2001). *Learning together: Peer tutoring in higher education.* London: Routledge Falmer.

Farrell, B., & Farrell, H. (2008). Student satisfaction with cooperative learning in an accounting curriculum. *Journal of University Teaching & Learning Practice, 5*(2), 40–54.

Fellingham, J. C. (2007). Is accounting an academic discipline? *Accounting Horizons, 21*(2), 159–163.

Geiger, M. A., & Ogilby, S. M. (2000). The first course in accounting: Students' perceptions and their effect on the decision to major in accounting. *Journal of Accounting Education, 18*(2), 63–78.

Ginsburg-Block, M. D., Rohrbeck, C. A., & Fantuzzo, J. W. (2006). A meta-analytic review of social, self-concept, and behavioral outcomes of peer-assisted learning. *Journal of Educational Psychology, 98*(4), 732–749.

Gist, W. E., Goedde, H., & Ward, B. H. (1996). The influence of mathematical skills and other factors on minority student performance in principles of accounting. *Issues in Accounting Education, 11*(1), 49–60.

Good, C., Aronson, J., & Inzlicht, M. (2003). Improving adolescents' standardized test performance: An intervention to reduce the effects of stereotype threat. *Journal of Applied Developmental Psychology, 24*(6), 645–662.

Gracia, L., & Jenkins, E. (2002). An exploration of student failure on an undergraduate accounting programme of study. *Accounting Education, 11*(1), 93–107.

Hartnett, N., Romcke, J., & Yap, C. (2004). Student performance in tertiary-level accounting: An international student focus. *Accounting & Finance, 44*(2), 163–185.

Hellstén, M. (2004). Learning at university: The international student experience. *International Education Journal, 5*(3), 344–351.

Hurtt, R. K., & Thomas, C. W. (2008). Implementing a required ethics class for students in accounting: The Texas experience. *Issues in Accounting Education, 23*(1), 31–51.

Jackling, B., & McDowall, T. (2008). Peer mentoring in an accounting setting: A case study of mentor skill development. *Accounting Education, 17*(4), 447–462.

Kulik, J. A., & Kulik, C. L. C. (1988). Timing of feedback and verbal learning. *Review of Educational Research, 58*(1), 79–97.

Lavoie, D., & Rosman, A. J. (2007). Using active student-centered learning-based instructional design to develop faculty and improve course design, delivery, and evaluation. *Issues in Accounting Education, 22*(1), 105–118.

Massey, D. W., & Van Hise, J. (2009). Walking the walk: Integrating lessons from multiple perspectives in the development of an accounting ethics course. *Issues in Accounting Education, 24*(4), 481–510.

Melé, D. (2005). Ethical education in accounting: Integrating rules, values, and virtues. *Journal of Business Ethics, 57*(1), 97–109.

Mowl, G., & Pain, R. (1995). Using self and peer assessment to improve students' essay writing: A case study from geography. *Programmed Learning, 32*(4), 324–335.

Packham, G., & Miller, C. (2000). Peer-assisted student support: A new approach to learning. *Journal of Further and Higher Education, 24*(1), 55–65.

Phillips, F., & Schmidt, R. N. (2010). Creating early success in financial accounting: Improving performance on adjusting journal entries. *Accounting Perspectives, 9*(2), 87–96.

Rankin, M., Silvester, M., Vallely, M., & Wyatt, A. (2003). An analysis of the implications of diversity for students' first level accounting performance. *Accounting & Finance, 43*(3), 365–393.

Richer, D. L. (1992). *The effects of two feedback systems on first year college students' writing proficiency.* Doctoral dissertation, University of Massachusetts, Lowell, MA.

Schroeder, N. W. (1986). Previous accounting education and college-level accounting exam performance. *Issues in Accounting Education, 1*(1), 37–47.

Topping, K. J. (1996). The effectiveness of peer tutoring in further and higher education: A typology and review of the literature. *Higher Education, 32*(3), 321–345.

Topping, K. J. (1998). Peer assessment between students in colleges and universities. *Review of Educational Research, 68*(3), 249–276.

Topping, K. J. (2005). Trends in peer learning. *Educational Psychology*, *25*(6), 631–645.

Tough, P. (2014). Who gets to graduate? *The New York Times*. Retrieved from http://www. nytimes.com/2014/05/18/magazine/who-gets-to-graduate.html?_r=0

Turner, L. E. (2006). Learning from accounting history: Will we get it right this time? *Issues in Accounting Education*, *21*(4), 383–407.

Van Lehn, K. A., Chi, M. T. H., Baggett, W., & Murray, R. C. (1995). *Progress report: Towards a theory of learning during tutoring*. Pittsburgh, PA: Learning Research and Development Center, University of Pittsburgh.

Vygotsky, L. S. (1980). *Mind in society: The development of higher psychological process*. Cambridge, MA: Harvard University Press.

Wilson, T. D., & Linville, P. W. (1982). Improving the academic performance of college freshmen: Attribution therapy revisited. *Journal of Personality and Social Psychology*, *42*(2), 367–376.

Wilson, T. D., & Linville, P. W. (1985). Improving the performance of college freshmen with attributional techniques. *Journal of Personality and Social Psychology*, *49*(1), 287–293.

Xiang, M., & Gruber, R. (2012). Student performance in their first post-secondary accounting course: Does high school accounting matter? *Advances in Accounting Education*, *13*, 297–311.

Yeager, D. S., & Walton, G. M. (2011). Social-psychological interventions in education: They're not magic. *Review of Educational Research*, *81*(2), 267–301.

REMOTE PROCTORING: THE EFFECT OF PROCTORING ON GRADES

Ann Boyd Davis, Richard Rand and Robert Seay

ABSTRACT

Purpose — *As more students take online courses as part of their college curricula, the integrity of testing in an online environment becomes increasingly important. The potential for cheating on exams is generally considered to be higher in an online environment. One approach to compensate for the absence of a physical proctor is to use a remote proctoring service that electronically monitors the student during the examination period.*

Methodology/approach — *We examined the exam grades for 261 students taking two different upper division accounting courses to determine if a computer-based remote proctoring service reduced the likelihood of cheating, measured through lower exam scores, as compared to classroom proctoring and no proctoring. We examined both online and on-campus courses.*

Findings — *In qualitative and quantitative accounting courses, evidence shows that grades were significantly lower for students who were proctored using a remote proctoring service compared to students who were*

Advances in Accounting Education: Teaching and Curriculum Innovations, Volume 18, 23–50
Copyright © 2016 by Emerald Group Publishing Limited
ISSN: 1085-4622/doi:10.1108/S1085-462220160000018002

not proctored. In the quantitative course, remote proctoring resulted in significantly lower final exam scores than either classroom or no proctoring. However, in the qualitative course, both remote proctoring online and live proctoring in a classroom resulted in significantly lower final exam scores than no proctoring, and they are not statistically different from each other.

Originality/value — *Academics and administrators should find these results helpful. The results suggest that the use of proctoring services in online courses has the potential to enhance the integrity of online courses by reducing the opportunities for academic dishonesty during exams.*

Keywords: Remote proctoring; online courses; cheating; exam grades; proctoring; accounting

The popularity of online education continues to trend upward as a majority of U.S. colleges and universities link plans for long-term success to online courses and program offerings (Allen & Seaman, 2014). The Babson Survey Research Group, led by Allen and Seaman, report that the 7.1 million students taking at least one online course during 2013 represent an all-time high for participation in online higher education. Even with recent declines in the rate of growth in online enrollment, multiple sources expect significant enrollment advances through the end of this decade (Allen & Seaman, 2014; Healy, 2014; Pappas, 2013).

Advocates for online higher education point to cost efficiencies and learning effectiveness as major benefits of an online platform. Businesses also recognize online training as a driver for improving competitive positions, reducing employee turnover, and generating higher employee productivity. The $56 billion e-Learning industry is expected to double by 2015, and a close working relationship between higher education and the business community is important to continuously improve the use of technology to acquire and disseminate knowledge (Pappas, 2013). However, higher education must deal with the unique challenges associated with the potential for academic dishonesty.

Academic dishonesty has been and will always be a matter of significant importance in the education community. The evolution of technology-driven learning in the college classroom presents multiple opportunities for students to engage in fraudulent submissions of homework, quizzes, and exams. How can an instructor be certain that the person taking an online exam is the enrolled student? How can the instructor determine if students do not prepare assignments and take exams in groups? How can the instructor know if the exam taker is using nonauthorized materials? Online course instructors routinely face these questions in the search for efficient and effective ways to detect or prevent acts of academic dishonesty. Answers are needed to satisfy the growing calls from college administrators and accrediting bodies to maintain the integrity of online courses.

A common element in many models that attempts to control for academic dishonesty includes proctored assignments and exams. This is usually not feasible for all graded activities, but there are many ways that proctoring could be used for significant graded course components: students could be required to attend a common proctored testing center(s); they could be required to come to campus to complete an assignment; or the instructor could use some form of remote proctoring software. The objectives of this chapter are to present how Tennessee Tech University uses a remote proctor service[1] in online upper division accounting courses and to determine if its use has any effect on final exam performance.

This study shows that, after controlling for other factors, the use of remote and classroom proctoring has a highly significant and negative effect on final exam performance. We also find that grade point average has a highly significant and positive relation with exam performance. For final exam grades, a prior bachelor's degree is highly significant and positive. In additional analyses, we examine the two different courses (Auditing and Cost Accounting) as proxies for qualitative and quantitative material, respectively. We find that both qualitative and quantitative final exam grades are negatively associated with remote proctoring indicating that remote proctoring's impact on exam grades as compared to no proctoring is not affected by the type of material tested in a course. However, for quantitative courses, classroom proctoring appears to be no different than no proctoring in online courses. Therefore, even for quantitative courses that are on campus, perhaps remote proctoring should be explored.

Overall, academics and administrators should find these results helpful as they suggest that the use of proctoring services in online courses has the potential to reduce the opportunities for academic dishonesty during exams. For online courses and programs to maintain integrity and meet the demands of accrediting bodies, the use of a remote proctoring service represents an attractive option. While Cluskey, Ehlen, and Raiborn (2011) introduce alternate methods of preventing and detecting academic dishonesty in situations where online proctoring does not occur, our chapter fills a gap in the literature by providing experience-based implementation guidance for remote proctoring and empirically demonstrating the statistical impact that remote proctoring has on final exam grades.

The remainder of the chapter is organized as follows. First, we discuss the background on remote proctoring. The following section provides an overview of the literature and hypothesis development. Finally, we present the sample, data, and model specification followed by the results and conclusions.

REMOTE PROCTORING

In two upper division accounting courses (Auditing and Cost Accounting), Tennessee Tech University used Remote Proctor NOW (RPN). RPN is a product of Software Secure, Inc., which has licensing agreements with over 200 colleges and universities. The Appendix provides information about RPN and other available remote proctoring products; however, this chapter does not evaluate the comparative features of these products.[2]

Instructors who adopt RPN must register each exam through the Software Secure website. Exam registration involves setting exam dates and times as well as identifying permitted and prohibited materials and activities. This includes the use of calculators, software, search engines, notes, books, etc.

To gain exam access, students log in to their Learning Management System (i.e., Desire 2 Learn, Blackboard) and then proceed to the course content area where a link to RPN has been created by the instructor. Students click on the link and immediately complete a system test for audio, video, and bandwidth requirements. After passing the system test, students download and install the RPN software, which must be done each time they take an exam.

The next step requires students to complete an identity verification interview that captures snapshots of the student and their university identification card. Students pan the entire testing room with their webcam to verify and document a clean testing environment. Approved course materials, if any, must also be clearly displayed and video recorded at this time. Finally, students are automatically directed to the textbook publisher's software (i.e., McGraw-Hill Connect, Cengage Mindtap, Pearson MyLab) login page to access the exam. Total preparation time from first login to starting the exam takes about 3−5 minutes.

The same instructor taught all courses included in this study and all exams were administered online regardless of whether the class was online or on campus. For the on-campus courses, students completed their exams in a centralized College of Business computer lab. The students took these exams at the same time, and the instructor proctored their work. For the online courses, the instructor allowed students to take their exams at any location where they had access to the Internet. Some of these courses were not proctored and some were proctored with RPN.

Generally, students must pay a fee online (currently $15) prior to being granted access to an exam. Acceptable forms of payment include credit cards, debit cards, and Pay Pal. In this study, the College of Business funded the entire cost.[3] The cost covers the use of the software and a thorough review by Software Secure of all audio, video, and computer screen recordings of the student during the exam. There are no additional costs to the colleges and universities that adopt RPN.

Software Secure offers instructor support during regular business hours and 24/7 student support. Instructors are encouraged to build practice exams at no cost to students that may be repeated an unlimited number of times. These are essential for both instructors and students as they begin the process of preparing and taking exams.

Software Secure's review team flags potential violations of exam rules directly on the recording meter, and instructors receive detailed reports within five business days of the exam date. Instructors have the option to view each student's recorded actions in real time or they may fast forward or replay the recordings as needed to determine if violations did, in fact, occur. During this study, RPN reported several instances of rules violations. In some cases, students briefly left the testing room, occasionally other individuals were in the general vicinity during the exam and, in one instance, a student used a headset while taking the exam. After a thorough review of each flagged incident, there was only one case of academic dishonesty that required disciplinary action. There were no cases of group test taking, all who took exams were enrolled students, and with the exception of one case, there were no unauthorized materials used during any of the exams. In the one case of academic dishonesty, the student was recorded searching the Internet for exam questions and solutions.

Implementation issues were often related to students not having adequate Internet connections, using outdated hardware and operating systems, and not completing practice exams. These problems became negligible as students gained experience with the product. In a very limited number of situations, students encountered technical problems that were attributable to RPN. In those cases, the instructor informed the students to bypass RPN and take their exam directly through the textbook publisher's software.

Data security is also a concern when investigating remote proctoring services. Instructors who plan to use remote proctoring should confirm if the selected vender is FERPA compliant. Software Secure reports they are FERPA compliant and imposes strict standards on security of personal and exam data.

PRIOR RESEARCH AND HYPOTHESIS DEVELOPMENT

Over the past 10 years, there has been mass migration of course availability from the traditional brick-and-mortar classroom to the Internet; however, the growth of online course delivery has brought with it several challenges. Those challenges include bridging the technology gap between students and faculty, moving content to an electronic format that can be delivered both synchronously and asynchronously, and establishing effective communication channels with students who an instructor may never actually meet. Notable among the challenges is the problem of ensuring the integrity of examinations that are completed by students who may not be in a secure location during the examination.

Imagine a student taking an online exam from a university located several hundreds of miles from the student's location. The student logs onto the internet at an appointed time to take an examination. The examination questions appear on the screen and the student proceeds to enter answers for those questions.

With online courses, faculty have a variety of concerns. Can the students effectively use the technology? How does the instructor know that the student is not using unauthorized aid in the process of answering those questions? How does the instructor know that the person entering answers is even the student registered for the course (Mallory, 2001)? In the end, how can the instructor assign a grade to the student, if the completion of the examination cannot be reliably traced back to the student?

To resolve these concerns, faculty face a limited number of options. The first option would simply be to do nothing; either assume the students are not going to cheat or ask them to sign a promise not to cheat, and hope they abide by their promise. Second, an instructor could depend upon "creative story-telling" and tell the students that they are being electronically proctored, when in fact they are not. Third, instructors may attempt to build in controls that "mimic" proctoring by making cheating much more difficult to accomplish. Cluskey et al. (2011) present a plan suggesting that adequate controls can be put in place to discourage cheating from occurring, even when students are not under the direct supervision of a proctor. Their controls include limiting the availability of an online exam, randomizing questions, randomizing the order of answers in objective questions, presenting questions one at a time, and allowing limited time for an exam. Watters, Robertson, and Clark (2011) found that randomization of questions is perceived by students to be the single most effective deterrent to cheating on online exams.

Fourth, some instructors will require all students, even those taking the classes remotely, to either come to the "home" campus to take their examinations or to arrange for a live proctoring service, such as at a local community college. This option is likely not going to be popular with students. University Business (2012) found that a majority of students (79 percent) taking courses remotely did not want to come to campus. Additionally, 77 percent of remote students take their online exams between 4:00 pm and midnight, while 48 percent took their exams on the weekends.

A final option exists in the form of a remote proctoring service. As stated earlier, remote proctoring usually involves some effort to identify that the person actually taking the exam and the enrolled student are one in the same. In addition, remote proctoring often involves some form of electronic surveillance of the student and/or the student's computer screen during the examination. In some cases, the remote proctoring is live, and at other times, the audio, visual, and screen-captured content can be archived for later retrieval. If the instructor manages the remote proctoring, then the instructor (or the instructor's agent) will have the responsibility to view the content to determine if cheating did in fact occur. Alternatively, the instructor can engage a remote proctoring service to capture all the relevant electronic data (audio, video, and screen-capture), review it, and report back to the instructor any "suspicious" activity. Ultimately, the decision to proctor or not to proctor will be driven by (1) whether cheating is actually going on in an online testing environment that is not proctored, and (2) whether proctoring in any form actually makes a difference.

Students certainly seem to think that cheating will be much easier online than in a traditional classroom. Watters et al. (2011) found that 46 percent of students reported that they had knowledge of other students receiving help with an online quiz or exam. Thirty-seven percent reported knowledge that other students had used prohibited materials on online quizzes or exams. In the various business disciplines, it was found that, overall, the degree of cheating was perceived to be least in accounting and greatest in management (Watters et al., 2011). In another study, students reported that they believed that the concept of academic integrity differs between the online environment and the classroom environment (Swartz & Cole, 2013).

Evidence appears to support student perceptions. Lanier (2006) found that 41.1 percent of students in online courses reported that they cheated, while only 20 percent reported cheating in traditional lecture courses. Nearly 40 percent admitted to assisting other students with cheating on online exams. Only 13.7 percent admitted to helping others cheat on exams in traditional lecture courses. Lanier (2006) also found that age and GPA are negatively correlated with cheating in an online environment. Finally, graduate students are less likely to cheat than undergraduate students.

Other studies contradict Lanier's finding on the higher prevalence of cheating in online classes. Watson and Sottile (2010) found, in an online survey, that 32.1 percent of students in a live classroom reported cheating while 32.7 percent of students in an online class reported cheating (the difference was not significant). Live classroom students did report, however, that they were more likely to be caught than online students, with 4.9 percent of the live classroom students reporting that they had been caught cheating compared to 2.1 percent of online students.

While much of the research in this area has focused on using surveys to examine the perception of the online testing environment, a few studies investigate the impact of remotely proctored online exams on cheating. Prince, Fulton, and Garsombke (2009) compared test scores of 76 graduate students who took proctored and nonproctored examinations. They found that test scores for proctored students were significantly lower on average than for students who were not proctored, by eight percentage points. In an economics class, Harmon and Lambrinos (2008) compared final exam scores in proctored and nonproctored settings to the scores of the other nonproctored exams in each setting. The results indicated that the proctored final exam scores were significantly lower than the other nonproctored exams for that class, while the nonproctored final exam scores were not significantly different than the other nonproctored exams for that class. While logic, and past research, would dictate that other factors may help to explain these differences, the only factor that appeared to be a statistically significant factor was GPA.

Confounding these findings is a 2012 study by Schultz, Shultz, and Schultz (2012) that found that students taking video monitored exams actually scored significantly higher (76.746) than students who took traditionally monitored exams (72.93). While the courses looked at in this study were online management courses, the authors reported the sample size to be "limited" (though the authors did not report the sample size). In addition, while the difference between groups was significant and positively correlated with video proctoring, the authors did not consider the actual difference to be impressive. Finally, the students in this study self-selected the testing environment, with cost being a major determinant for the majority of students who chose to be tested in the traditional environment.

If the use of remote proctoring results in a negative change in exam grades, the question arises as to whether this indicates that the negative decline in exam grades is resultant of a lower level of cheating or is the negative bias introduced by the technology. Anakwe (2008) found that, in a comparison of student performance in paper-based versus computer-based testing, there was no significant difference between the two methods of testing. Bugbee (1996) found similar results. In addition, Bugbee found that, when the exams are exactly the same, the results are even stronger that there are no differences in performance. Alternatively, Brallier, Maguire, Palm, and Smith (2010) tested 179 Intermediate Accounting I students and found that students taking a computer-based test scored significantly higher than students taking the same test in a pencil-and-paper format.

Given the limited number of studies that have investigated the effect of proctoring on exam grades in an online environment and the contradictory results in these findings, the impact of proctoring on exam grades given different settings is an empirical question. Although we do not expect a positive relation with proctoring and exam grades, it is possible that proctoring has no discernible effect on exam grades, particularly when examining the difference in an online versus classroom proctoring experience and given the use of technology. However, the goal of proctoring, in any format, is to discourage cheating. Based on the prior discussion, we hypothesize the following:

H1. Remote proctoring is negatively associated with final exam grades.

SAMPLE, DATA, AND MODEL SPECIFICATION

Sample

To investigate the association between exam grades and the type of proctoring, we collect and analyze data on 261 students from 2012 to 2014. The primary sample consists of final exam grades from 244 students with a supplemental sample including midterm grades from 149 students. While the main analysis includes 244 student-observations from both Auditing and Cost Accounting courses, the supplemental sample of midterm grades includes only student-observations from the Auditing course. We gathered all of the student information by analyzing student transcript information through the Tennessee Tech University system.

Data and Model Specification

We employ the following ordinary least squares regression model to investigate the relation between exam grades and the type of proctoring:

$$
\begin{aligned}
EXAMGRADE_i = {} & \alpha_0 + \beta_1 PROCTOR\_Remote_i + \beta_2 PROCTOR\_Class_i \\
& + \beta_3 COURSE_i + \beta_4 GPA_i + \beta_5 THRS_i + \beta_6 REPEAT_i \\
& + \beta_7 FTPT_i + \beta_8 DEGREE_i + \beta_9 AGE_i + \beta_{10} GENDER_i + \varepsilon_i
\end{aligned}
$$

$EXAMGRADE$ is the final exam grade from student i. We generate binary variables for all three of the possible types of proctoring. We classify each student-observation into one of the following three groups: (1) $PROCTOR\_Remote$: students taking an online course using remote proctoring, (2) $PROCTOR\_Class$: students taking an on-campus course using classroom proctoring, and (3) $PROCTOR\_No$: students taking an online course using no proctoring. We leave the last group in the intercept. To test $H1$, the impact of remote proctoring as compared to no proctoring, β_1 will be negative if students receive lower exam grades given remote proctoring and in comparison to the traditional no proctoring in online classes. Furthermore, to examine the difference in remote proctoring and classroom proctoring, we will test the difference in β_1 and β_2. We define all variables in Table 1.

The control variables for the above model are developed from Seay and Milkman (1994) and Rudolph, Seay, and Milkman (2000). These models were originally used in analyzing the effectiveness of interactive television instructional programing and have been adapted to this setting using remote proctoring for exams. The first control variable captures course characteristics. Here we include a variable ($COURSE$) to control for the data containing two different courses (Auditing and Cost Accounting). $COURSE$ is equal to 1 for the Auditing Course. We also include this control as Cost Accounting tends to represent a quantitative course and Audit serves as a qualitative course. We do not predict direction on this variable as we are exploring the association here.

Table 1. Variable Definitions and Data Sources.

Variable	Definitions and Data Sources (in Parentheses)
Dependent variable	
EXAMGRADE	Final exam grade of a student
Independent variable	
PROCTOR_Remote	Indicator variable coded 1 if remote proctoring and 0 otherwise
PROCTOR_Class	Indicator variable coded 1 if classroom proctoring and 0 otherwise
PROCTOR_No	Indicator variable coded 1 if no proctoring and 0 otherwise
Control variables	
COURSE	Indicator variable coded 1 for the Auditing Course (ACCT3620) and 0 for the Cost Accounting Course (ACCT3210)
GPA	Cumulative GPA for a student immediately prior to taking the course
THRS	Total earned hours for a student immediately prior to taking the course
REPEAT	Indicator variable coded 1 for repeating the course containing the exam and 0 for no repeat
FTPT	Indicator variable coded 1 for a full-time student in the semester taking the course containing the exam and 0 for a part-time student
DEGREE	Indicator variable coded 1 for holding a Bachelor's degree prior to taking the course containing the exam and 0 for no Bachelor's degree
AGE	Age of student in the semester taking the course containing the exam
GENDER	Indicator variable coded 1 for male and 0 for female

Next, we include variables to control for student academic characteristics. First, we control for a student's cumulative GPA immediately prior to taking the observed course (*GPA*). Consistent with Harmon and Lambrinos (2008), we expect that increases in GPA will likely be associated with increased exam grades. This variable captures the overall academic performance of the student. *THRS* controls for the total earned hours for a student immediately prior to taking the observed course. We expect a positive association between total earned hours and exam grades as the higher hours likely proxy for academic experience or maturity. Unlike Harmon and Lambrinos (2008), we use total earned hours rather than class rank to control for academic experience or maturity and predict a positive association. We argue that total earned hours is a more precise measure than class rank. To control for the potential to retake a course, we include *REPEAT* equal to 1 for repeating the course. We expect that *REPEAT* will have a positive association with exam grades as a student is more familiar with the material and knows the professor's teaching style. A student can take a full-time or part-time course load; therefore, we control for the course load the student is taking in the semester the student takes the observed course (*FTPT*). Here, we code *FTPT* as 1 for full-time. We define a full-time load as 12 credit-hours for the Fall and Spring semesters and six credit-hours for the Summer semester. Given that time is a constraint that can impact performance, we expect a negative association with course load and exam grades. Lastly, we control for whether the student holds a Bachelor's degree prior to taking the observed course (*DEGREE*). *DEGREE* is equal to 1 if the student holds a Bachelor's degree. Having a prior Bachelor's degree should be positively associated with higher exam grades as students have demonstrated the ability to complete a program and have strong academic performance.

The last group of variables includes student personal characteristics. We control for the age of a student (*AGE*). Consistent with Harmon and Lambrinos (2008), we do not predict a directional association with age and exam grades. While an increase in age might result in higher exam grades due to maturity and a greater commitment to academic achievement, an increase in age might also result in lower exam grades resulting from additional obligations and commitments in life that can come with age (i.e., family, job). The model also includes *GENDER* coded as 1 for male. Here, we make no prediction about how gender will impact exam grades. We employ robust standard errors in all specifications. While we do not formally lag any of our variables, we are careful to collect many of the student academic characteristics immediately prior to taking the observed course.

RESULTS

Descriptive Statistics and Correlations

In Table 2, Panel A presents descriptive statistics of the variables from the 244 observations. The average final exam grade (*EXAMGRADE*) across our sample is 76.6. The sample consists of approximately 23 percent remote proctored observations (*PROCTOR_Remote*), 35 percent classroom proctored (*PROCTOR_Class*), and 43 percent no proctored (*PROCTOR_No*). In untabulated results, the average midterm exam grade is 79.3. Again, we only captured the midterm grades for the Auditing class and this sample contains 149 observations. While the overall exam scores (midterm and final) for the student-observations taking the Auditing course (79.3 and 76.97, respectively) are not statistically significant, we do find significance when we use a controlled limited sample. During the Fall 2013 semester, students enrolled in the online Auditing course were given a midterm exam with no proctoring and a final exam using remote proctoring. For the mid-term exam, there were 17 student-observations with an exam average of 85.2. However, for the final exam, there were 13 student-observations with a significantly lower exam average of 69.2 (*p-value* < *0.01*).[4] As this sample controls for the type of proctoring, we conclude that this finding provides preliminary support for *H1*.

Over 60 percent of the observations relate to the Auditing course (*COURSE*). Based on the sample, the students have an average GPA of 2.902 (*GPA*) and have taken approximately 64 credit-hours prior to enrolling in the observed course (*THRS*). Only 4 percent of the sample chose to retake either the Cost Accounting or Auditing course. Over 78 percent of the students are enrolled in full-time class loads. Again, a full-time load consists of six credit-hours in the Summer semester and 12 credit-hours in the Fall and Spring semester. Only 17 percent of the sample has a Bachelor's degree prior to taking the observed courses. The average age of our enrolled students for these observed courses is 28 years with slightly more than 50 percent of the students being male (59 percent).

In Table 2, Panel B shows descriptive statistics for the 244 observations by independent variable. The average final exam for the *PROCTOR_Remote* observations is 67.1 with the average final exam for *PROCTOR_Class* and *PROCTOR_No* equal to 75.6 and 82.5, respectively. *PROCTOR_Remote* average final exam is statistically lower than both of the other exam scores, providing univariate support for *H1*.

Table 3 provides correlation coefficients for the variables. Similar to other research, we examine the independent variables to ensure that they are not so highly correlated that their independent effects in the regression model cannot be determined. Using Pearson correlations, the highest correlation magnitudes between independent variables are −0.480 between *AGE* and *FTPT*, −0.475 between *DEGREE* and *THRS*, and 0.416 between *DEGREE* and *AGE*. All other pairwise correlations are below 0.400. Therefore, collinearity in the data does not appear to be of major concern.

Regression Results

We present the results from the main regression model in Table 4. As expected, both *PROCTOR_Remote* and *PROCTOR_Class* have a negative and significant impact on final exam grades (coefficient = −0.1520, *t*-stat = −6.26 and coefficient = −0.0895, *t*-stat = −3.55, respectively). Relative to student observations with no proctoring (the group in the intercept),

Table 2. Descriptive Statistics, 2012–2014.

Panel A: Total 244 observations

Variables	Mean	Std. Dev.	Minimum	Median	Maximum
Dependent variable					
EXAMGRADE	0.766	0.164	0.000	0.800	1.000
Independent variable					
PROCTOR_Remote	0.225	0.419	0.000	0.000	1.000
PROCTOR_Class	0.348	0.477	0.000	0.000	1.000
PROCTOR_No	0.426	0.496	0.000	0.000	1.000
Control variables					
COURSE	0.607	0.490	0.000	1.000	1.000
GPA	2.902	1.004	0.000	3.125	4.000
THRS	63.780	42.696	0.000	69.000	207.000
REPEAT	0.041	0.199	0.000	0.000	1.000
FTPT	0.783	0.413	0.000	1.000	1.000
DEGREE	0.172	0.378	0.000	0.000	1.000
AGE	27.570	7.273	20.000	24.000	58.000
GENDER	0.586	0.494	0.000	1.000	1.000

Panel B: Observations by independent variable

Variables	PROCTOR_Remote 55 Obs	PROCTOR_Class 85 Obs	PROCTOR_No 104 Obs	Remote vs. _Class t-test	Remote vs. _No t-test
Dependent variable					
EXAMGRADE	0.671	0.756	0.825	−2.866***	−6.577***
Control variables					
COURSE	0.527	0.694	0.577	−2.010**	−0.597
GPA	2.658	3.218	2.773	−3.564***	−0.598
THRS	42.490	79.588	62.118	−6.237***	−2.653***
REPEAT	0.018	0.024	0.067	−0.212	−1.347
FTPT	0.636	0.953	0.721	−5.284***	−1.099
DEGREE	0.273	0.012	0.250	5.136***	0.310
AGE	28.673	24.271	29.683	3.900***	−0.776
GENDER	0.655	0.529	0.596	1.465	0.717

Notes: ***, **, and * indicate significance for a two-tailed test at the 1 percent, 5 percent, and 10 percent levels, respectively. See Table 1 for variable definitions.

Table 3. Correlation Coefficients, 2012–2014 (*N* = 244 Observations).

Variables	EXAM GRADE	PROCTOR_Remote	PROCTOR_Class	PROCTOR_No	COURSE	GPA
EXAM GRADE	1.000	−0.319	−0.025	0.294	0.041	0.254
		<0.01	0.69	<0.01	0.53	<0.01
PROCTOR_Remote	−0.314	1.000	−0.394	−0.465	−0.088	−0.055
	<0.01		<0.01	<0.01	0.17	0.40
PROCTOR_Class	−0.046	−0.394	1.000	−0.630	0.131	0.182
	0.47	<0.01		<0.01	0.04	<0.01
PROCTOR_No	0.310	−0.465	−0.630	1.000	−0.052	−0.129
	<0.01	<0.01	<0.01		0.42	0.04
COURSE	0.027	−0.088	0.131	−0.052	1.000	0.002
	0.67	0.17	0.04	0.42		0.98
GPA	0.277	−0.131	0.231	−0.111	0.012	1.000
	<0.01	0.04	<0.01	0.08	0.85	
THRS	0.115	−0.270	0.271	−0.034	0.149	0.372
	0.07	<0.01	<0.01	0.60	0.02	<0.01
REPEAT	−0.038	−0.062	−0.064	0.114	0.082	−0.067
	0.55	0.33	0.32	0.07	0.20	0.30
FTPT	0.092	−0.192	0.302	−0.129	−0.078	0.303
	0.15	<0.01	<0.01	0.04	0.22	<0.01
DEGREE	0.082	0.144	−0.311	0.178	−0.033	−0.198
	0.20	0.02	<0.01	0.01	0.61	<0.01
AGE	−0.022	0.082	−0.332	0.251	−0.020	−0.128
	0.73	0.20	<0.01	<0.01	0.76	0.05
GENDER	0.010	0.075	−0.084	0.018	−0.030	−0.076
	0.87	0.24	0.19	0.78	0.65	0.23

Variables	THRS	REPEAT	FTPT	DEGREE	AGE	GENDER
EXAM GRADE	0.117	−0.003	0.087	0.069	0.049	0.034
	0.07	0.96	0.17	0.28	0.44	0.59
PROCTOR_Remote	−0.285	−0.062	−0.192	0.144	0.029	0.075
	<0.01	0.33	<0.01	0.02	0.66	0.24
PROCTOR_Class	0.287	−0.064	0.302	−0.311	−0.441	−0.084
	<0.01	0.32	<0.01	<0.01	<0.01	0.19
PROCTOR_No	−0.036	0.114	−0.129	0.178	0.401	0.018
	0.58	0.07	0.04	0.01	<0.01	0.78
COURSE	0.181	0.082	−0.078	−0.033	−0.048	−0.030
	<0.01	0.20	0.22	0.61	0.45	0.65
GPA	0.208	−0.138	0.148	−0.096	−0.160	−0.146
	<0.01	0.03	0.02	0.14	0.01	0.02
THRS	1.000	−0.022	0.324	−0.473	−0.220	−0.001
		0.74	<0.01	<0.01	<0.01	0.99
REPEAT	−0.031	1.000	−0.042	−0.040	0.123	0.048
	0.64		0.52	0.54	0.06	0.46
FTPT	0.304	−0.042	1.000	−0.313	−0.429	−0.100
	<0.01	0.52		<0.01	<0.01	0.12
DEGREE	−0.475	−0.040	−0.313	1.000	0.457	0.075
	<0.01	0.54	<0.01		<0.01	0.25
AGE	−0.195	0.084	−0.480	0.416	1.000	0.022
	<0.01	0.19	<0.01	<0.01		0.73
GENDER	−0.010	0.048	−0.100	0.075	−0.030	1.000
	0.88	0.46	0.12	0.25	0.64	

Notes: Spearman (Pearson) correlation coefficients are shown in the upper (lower) diagonals. Two-tailed *p*-values are shown below the correlation coefficients. See Table 1 for variable definitions.

student observations with both remote and classroom proctoring have significantly lower final exam grades. This finding supports *H1* in that remote proctoring is statistically significant and negative in comparison to no proctoring. Furthermore, when testing the difference between *PROCTOR_Remote* and *PROCTOR_Class*, we find that the two are statistically different (*F*-stat = 4.40).

This finding supports the idea that remote proctoring is more stringent than classroom proctoring, particularly in light of the online and classroom exams all being given in a digital teaching and learning environment (i.e., McGraw-Hill Connect, Cengage Mindtap, Pearson MyLab). In other words, the remote proctoring directly monitors each individual taking an exam rather than one instructor monitoring an entire classroom in classroom proctoring. As stated earlier, prior research indicates that the lower exam scores are not related to effects of the technology. To the contrary, these effects may be due to a lower incidence of academic dishonesty. For example, PRNewswire (2014) reported 2,500 students taking final examinations using the Examity remote proctoring service. They only observed seven students cheating, a rate of only .28 percent. This is materially lower than the self-reported cheating rate of over 40 percent reported by Lanier (2006) and others. We believe this finding to be highly important as education continues to move to online delivery. Overall, these results further corroborate our findings in Table 4.

GPA is highly significant and positive, indicating that an increase in the student's average GPA is associated with an increase in the final exam grade (coefficient = 0.0479, *t*-stat = 4.57). *DEGREE* is positively associated with the final exam grade (coefficient = 0.0713, *t*-stat = 2.75), indicating that students with a prior bachelor's degree perform better on the final exam. This variable could perhaps be a proxy for maturity.

Additional Analyses

Regression Analysis without PROCTOR_No
To further investigate the difference in the coefficients of *PROCTOR_Remote* and *PROCTOR_Class*, we drop all the observations with no proctoring (*PROCTOR_No*). Therefore, we are left with observations that have either remote or classroom proctoring. In Table 5, Column A, *PROCTOR_Remote* is equal to 1 for remote proctoring observations and 0 otherwise, with *PROCTOR_Class* being omitted from the model and going through the intercept. In this model, *PROCTOR_Remote* is highly

Table 4. Regression Model for EXAMGRADE.

$EXAMGRADE_i = \alpha_0 + \beta_1 PROCTOR\_Remote_i + \beta_2 PROCTOR\_Class_i$
$+ \beta_3 COURSE_i + \beta_4 GPA_i + \beta_5 THRS_i + \beta_6 REPEAT_i$
$+ \beta_7 FTPT_i + \beta_8 DEGREE_i + \beta_9 AGE_i + \beta_{10} GENDER_i + \varepsilon_i$

Variables	Predicted Direction	Coeff.	t-Stat
Independent variable			
PROCTOR_Remote	−	−0.1520	−6.26***
PROCTOR_Class	−	−0.0895	−3.55***
Control variables			
COURSE	+/−	0.0099	0.53
GPA	+	0.0479	4.57***
THRS	+	0.0001	0.35
REPEAT	+	−0.0394	−0.54
FTPT	−	0.0040	0.14
DEGREE	+	0.0713	2.75***
AGE	+/−	−0.0021	−1.36
GENDER	+/−	0.0097	0.62
Intercept		0.7190	10.31***
N		244	
F-stat		8.48	
R^2		0.237	
Test			
PROCTOR_Remote = PROCTOR_Class			
F-stat		4.40**	

Notes: ***, **, and * indicate significance for a two-tailed test at the 1 percent, 5 percent, and 10 percent levels, respectively. See Table 1 for variable definitions.

significant and negative indicating that the final exam is significantly lower for remote proctoring as compared to classroom proctoring. In Table 5, Column B, *PROCTOR_Class* is equal to 1 for classroom proctoring observations and 0 otherwise. Again, *PROCTOR_Class* is highly significant and positive indicating that the final exam is significantly higher for classroom proctoring as compared to remote proctoring. The control variables in both models are consistent with Table 4. Overall, this finding is consistent with the main analysis. From here, we conclude that, on average, final exam grades are lower for remote proctoring as compared to classroom proctoring.

Course and Midterm Exam Grades
As previously mentioned, the final exam data includes grades from both Auditing and Cost Accounting courses. The objectives of many Auditing

Table 5.   Regression Model Excluding PROCTOR_No.

Variables	Predicted direction	Column A: PROCTOR_Remote Coeff.	t-stat	Column B: PROCTOR_Class Coeff.	t-stat
Independent variable					
PROCTOR_Remote	−	−0.0669	−1.98**		
PROCTOR_Class	+			0.0669	1.98***
Control variables					
COURSE	+/−	−0.0032	−0.12	−0.0032	−0.12
GPA	+/−	0.0697	4.70***	0.0697	4.70***
THRS	+	0.0002	0.50	0.0002	0.50
REPEAT	+	−0.1836	−0.95	−0.1836	−0.95
FTPT	+	0.0144	0.31	0.0144	0.31
DEGREE	−	0.1237	2.85***	0.1237	2.85***
AGE	+	0.0003	0.13	0.0003	0.13
GENDER	+/−	−0.0106	−0.37	−0.0106	−0.37
Intercept	+/−	0.5029	4.78***	0.4360	4.17***
N		140		140	
F-stat		4.83		4.83	
R^2		0.2583		0.2583	

Notes: In this model, all the no proctored observations are dropped. In Column A, PROCTOR_Remote is an indicator variable coded as 1 for remote proctoring and 0 otherwise. In Column B, PROCTOR_Class is an indicator variable coded as 1 for classroom proctoring and 0 otherwise. ***, **, and * indicate significance for a two-tailed test at the 1 percent, 5 percent, and 10 percent levels, respectively. See Table 1 for variable definitions.

courses include describing the nature of an audit, distinguishing between the types of audit reports, differentiating between the role of management and the role of the auditor in the preparation of the financial statements, and analyzing the concept of materiality in an audit. All of these objectives relate to qualitative characteristics. On the other hand, the objectives of Cost Accounting include identifying and calculating different types of costs, distinguishing between job-costing, process-costing, and joint-costing systems, and determining the product cost by means of full-costing and direct-costing methods. These objectives tend to relate more to quantitative characteristics. Therefore, we run the model by *COURSE* (Table 6, Columns A and B) to test whether proctoring impacts final exam grades in qualitative classes (Auditing course) differently than quantitative classes (Cost Accounting course).

As shown in Table 6 (Columns A and B), *PROCTOR_Remote* is highly significant and negatively associated with final exam grades in both

Table 6. Regression Model for EXAMGRADE by COURSE and Using MidTerm Exam Grades.

$$EXAMGRADE_i = \alpha_0 + \beta_1 PROCTOR\_Remote_i + \beta_2 PROCTOR\_Class_i + \beta_3 COURSE_i + \beta_4 GPA_i + \beta_5 THRS_i + \beta_6 REPEAT_i + \beta_7 FTPT_i + \beta_8 DEGREE_i + \beta_9 AGE_i + \beta_{10} GENDER_i + \varepsilon_i$$

Variables	Predicted direction	Column A: Final Exam Grade Auditing (Qualitative)		Column B: Final Exam Grade Cost Accounting (Quantitative)		Column C: Midterm Exam Grade Auditing (Qualitative)	
		Coeff.	t-stat	Coeff.	t-stat	Coeff.	t-stat
Independent variable							
PROCTOR_Remote	−	−0.1490	−4.66***	−0.1552	−4.17***	−0.0631	−2.10**
PROCTOR_Class	−	−0.1344	−4.15***	−0.0086	−0.23	−0.1044	−3.61***
Control variables							
COURSE	+/−						
GPA	+	0.0500	3.31***	0.0493	3.26***	0.0320	2.46**
THRS	+	−0.0001	−0.19	0.0003	0.79	−0.0003	−1.34
REPEAT	+	−0.0554	−0.62	0.0314	0.42	−0.0298	−0.48
FTPT	−	0.0078	0.20	0.0031	0.07	−0.0001	0.00
DEGREE	+	0.0358	1.00	0.1204	3.13***	−0.0033	−0.12
AGE	+/−	−0.0030	−1.55	−0.0002	−0.08	−0.0021	−1.36
GENDER	+/−	0.0163	0.64	0.0180	0.55	0.0343	1.54
Intercept		0.7770	8.79***	0.6150	5.88***	0.8089	12.27***
N		148		96		149	
F-stat		5.53		5.52		3.14	
R^2		0.2401		0.3152		0.1547	
PROCTOR_Remote = PROCTOR_Class test F-stat		0.14		10.01***		1.78	

Notes: ***, **, and * indicate significance for a two-tailed test at the 1 percent, 5 percent, and 10 percent levels, respectively. See Table 1 for variable definitions.

qualitative (Column A: Auditing, coefficient = −0.1490, t-stat = −4.66) and quantitative courses (Column B: Cost Accounting, coefficient = −0.1552, t-stat = −4.17). However, *PROCTOR_Class* is only highly significant and negative in qualitative courses (Column A: Auditing, coefficient = −0.1344, t-stat = −4.15). Interestingly, when examining the difference in the coefficients of *PROCTOR_Remote* and *PROCTOR_Class*, the two are not statistically different for qualitative courses (Auditing) but are statistically different with remote proctoring being significantly lower for quantitative courses (Cost Accounting). Consistent with the main analysis for final exam grades, *GPA* is highly significant and positive across both Auditing and Cost Accounting courses. However, *DEGREE* is highly significant and positive in Cost Accounting final exam grades and is not a significant predictor of Auditing final exam grades.

In a consistent method, we examine midterm exam grades and find that these have similar results to the Auditing final exam grades. Perhaps this finding is consistent given that the midterm grades are comprised solely of Auditing observations. Again, *PROCTOR_Remote* and *PROCTOR_Class* are both highly significant and negative when compared to no proctoring; however, remote and classroom proctoring are not statistically different.

Based on this analysis, we conclude that the use of remote proctoring is important in an online course regardless of the type of course (qualitative and quantitative) and produces lower exam grades than no proctoring. In qualitative courses (Auditing), remote proctoring for online courses is not different from the traditional classroom proctoring. However, in quantitative courses (Cost Accounting), the use of classroom proctoring may not be adequate because we find that classroom proctoring is not statistically different from no proctoring. Therefore, if the course is quantitative in nature, perhaps remote proctoring should be used in place of traditional classroom proctoring for on-campus classes. We also note that inferences drawn from this analysis should be interpreted with caution because the sample sizes are relatively small.

Proctoring versus No Proctoring

To validate our main result in final exam grades that increasing proctoring results in lower exam grades, we examine proctoring, combining remote and classroom proctoring, versus no proctoring. We include descriptive statistics, including t-tests, in Table 7, Panel A. Here, consistent with the main analysis, 140 observations represent proctoring and 104 observations represent no proctoring with the average final exam grades equal to 72.2 and 82.5 for the respective groups. The t-test of the average final exam grades is

Table 7. Descriptive Statistics and Regression Model for Proctoring versus No Proctoring.

Panel A: Descriptive statistics (n = 244)

Variables	PROCTOR_Class & _Remote	PROCTOR_No	Proctoring versus No Proctoring	
	140 Obs	104 Obs	Diff	t-test
Dependent variable				
EXAMGRADE	0.722	0.825	-0.102	-5.067***
Control variables				
COURSE	0.629	0.577	0.052	0.815
GPA	2.998	2.773	0.225	1.741*
THRS	65.014	62.118	2.896	0.523
REPEAT	0.021	0.067	-0.046	-1.792*
FTPT	0.829	0.721	0.107	2.021**
DEGREE	0.114	0.250	-0.136	-2.811***
AGE	26.000	29.683	-3.683	-4.032***
GENDER	0.579	0.596	-0.018	-0.275

Panel B: Regression model

$$EXAMGRADE_i = \alpha_0 + \beta_1 PROCTOR + \beta_2 COURSE_i + \beta_3 GPA_i + \beta_4 THRS_i + \beta_5 REPEAT_i + \beta_6 FTPT_i + \beta_7 DEGREE_i + \beta_8 AGE_i + \beta_9 GENDER_i + \varepsilon_i$$

Variables	Predicted Direction	Coeff.	t-Stat
Independent variable			
PROCTOR	-	-0.1176	-5.89***
Control variables			
COURSE	+/-	0.0149	0.76
GPA	+	0.0495	4.78***
THRS	+	0.0002	0.75

Table 7. (*Continued*)

Panel B: Regression model

$$EXAMGRADE_i = \alpha_0 + \beta_1 PROCTOR + \beta_2 COURSE_i + \beta_3 GPA_i + \beta_4 THRS_i + \beta_5 REPEAT_i + \beta_6 FTPT_i + \beta_7 DEGREE_i + \beta_8 AGE_i + \beta_9 GENDER_i + \varepsilon_i$$

Variables	Predicted Direction	Coeff.	*t*-Stat
REPEAT	+	−0.0373	−0.53
FTPT	−	0.0123	0.42
DEGREE	+	0.0670	2.60***
AGE	+/−	−0.0024	−1.57
GENDER	+/−	0.0065	0.33
Intercept		0.7116	9.93***
N		244	
F-stat		8.18	
R^2		0.2205	

Notes: PROCTOR is an indicator variable defined as 1 for remote and classroom proctoring and 0 for no proctoring. ***, **, and * indicate significance for a two-tailed test at the 1 percent, 5 percent, and 10 percent levels, respectively. See Table 1 for variable definitions.

statistically significant with the proctored grades being significantly lower. In Table 7, Panel B, we show the regression results. Consistent with the main results, proctoring is highly significant and negative indicating that as proctoring increases final exam grades decline. *GPA* and *DEGREE* are also highly significant and positive. Overall, these results support our findings in Table 4.[5]

CONCLUSION

The purposes of our chapter are to provide experience-based implementation guidance for remote proctoring and to empirically demonstrate the statistical impact that proctoring has on exam grades. We contribute to the literature by detailing the process for implementation of a remote proctoring system. Furthermore, in an accounting setting, we provide empirical evidence that remote and classroom proctoring have a highly significant and negative relation with both final exam and midterm exam grades. In additional analyses, we examine Auditing and Cost Accounting final exam grades separately as proxies for qualitative and quantitative material, respectively. Here, we find that both qualitative and quantitative final exam grades are negatively associated with remote proctoring indicating that remote proctoring's impact on exam grades as compared to no proctoring is not affected by the type of material tested in a course. However, for quantitative courses, classroom proctoring appears to be no different than no proctoring in online courses. Therefore, for on-campus classes that are quantitative, perhaps remote proctoring should be explored.

Given the popularity of online education and the expected rise in enrollment through the end of this decade coupled with the propensity to engage in fraudulent activity in an online, technology-driven learning environment, the practical application and use of RPN, or other remote proctoring services should be of interest to academics entering and thriving in the world of online education. Administrators and accrediting agencies should also consider the impact that proctoring has on final exam grades. Specifically, we find that remote proctoring has approximately a 15.20 percentage point decline in final exam grades. Overall, academics and administrators should find these results helpful as the findings suggest that the use of proctoring services in online courses has the potential to reduce the opportunities for academic dishonesty during exams.

While we do find a highly statistical and negative relation with remote and classroom proctoring and exam grades, our results are based on student-observations from 2012 to 2014. Our results are also specific to accounting and examine only two courses within accounting. Future research should broaden the sample to continue to examine this relation as remote proctoring becomes more prevalent in online courses.

NOTES

1. Tennessee Tech University used Remote Proctor NOW for its online remote proctoring service.

2. The authors and this journal are not endorsing the use of RPN or any other remote proctoring service.

3. Subsequent to this experiment, students have paid for the use of RPNow without resistance. However, students have not been asked to pay for more than two exams in a single course. Pushback might occur if a class requires more than two remote proctored exams. The $15 cost per exam has not changed and is current as of March 2015. Current plans are to continue requiring the student to be responsible for the costs of remote proctoring services.

4. We used a t-test to examine the difference resulting in a t-statistic of 3.7245. To resolve any concern that the dependent variable is not a normally distributed interval variable, we also used the nonparametric Wilcoxon-Mann-Whitney test resulting in a z-statistic of 3.062 (p-value < 0.01).

5. We would like to thank an anonymous reviewer for highlighting this concern.

ACKNOWLEDGMENTS

We appreciate the helpful comments of Timothy J. Rupert (editor) and two anonymous reviewers. We gratefully acknowledge the helpful feedback provided by participants at the 2015 American Accounting Association Southeast Region Meeting. We also appreciate the research assistance of Matthew Coats and Katy Boles Miller.

REFERENCES

Allen, I. E., & Seaman, J. (2014). Grade change: Tracking online education in the United States. Babson Park, MA: Babson Survey Research Group.

Anakwe, B. (2008). Comparison of student performance in paper-based versus computer-based testing. *Journal of Education for Business*, *84*(1), 13–17.

Brallier, S. A., Maguire, K. A., Palm, L. J., & Smith, D. A. (2010). Computer-based testing: A comparison of computer-based and paper-and-pencil assessment. *Academy of Educational Leadership Journal, 14*(4), 117–225.

Bugbee, A. C., Jr. (1996). The equivalence of paper-and-pencil and computer-based testing. *Journal of Research on Computing in Education, 28*(3), 282–299.

Cluskey, G. R., Jr., Ehlen, C. R., & Raiborn, M. H. (2011). Thwarting online exam cheating without proctor supervision. *Journal of Academic and Business Ethics, 4*(July), 1.

Harmon, O. R., & Lambrinos, J. (2008). Are online exams an invitation to cheat? *Journal of Economic Education, 39*(2), 116–125.

Healy, F. (2014). *Online degree courses lose momentum.* Higher Ed Growth, February. Retrieved from http://www.higheredgrowth.com/online-degree-courses-lose-momentum/

Lanier, M. M. (2006). Academic integrity and distance learning. *Journal of Criminal Justice Education, 17*(October), 244–261.

Mallory, J. R. (2001). Adequate testing and evaluation of on-line learners. *Instructional Technology and Education of the Deaf Symposium Proceedings*, June. Retrieved from http://www.rit.edu/~w-tecsym/papers/2001/M230A.pdf

Pappas, C. (2013). *Top 10-eLearning statistics for 2014 infographic.* eLearning Industry, December. Retrieved from http://elearningindustry.com/top-10-e-learning-statistics-for-2014-you-need-to-know

Prince, D. J., Fulton, R. A., & Garsombke, T. W. (2009). Comparisons of proctored versus non-proctored testing strategies in graduate distance education curriculum. *Journal of College Teaching and Learning, 6*(November), 51–62.

PRNewswire. (2014). *Technology-based online proctoring sharply reduces cheating on college finals.* January. Retrieved from http://www.prnewswire.com/news-releases/technology-based-online-proctoring-sharply-reduces-cheating-on-college-finals-239058501.html

Rudolph, H. R., Seay, R. A., & Milkman, M. I. (2000). Assessing the effectiveness of interactive television instruction in an upper division accounting course. *Advances in Accounting Education, 3*, 151–168.

Schultz, M. C., Shultz, J. T., & Schultz, J. J. (2012). An evaluation of examination results between students in management courses being video monitored verses those in a traditionally monitored environment. *The Business Review, Cambridge, 20*, 76–82.

Seay, R. A., & Milkman, M. I. (1994). Interactive television instruction: An assessment of student performance and attitudes in an upper division accounting course. *Issues in Accounting Education, 9*(1), 80–95.

Swartz, L. B., & Cole, M. T. (2013). Students' perception of academic integrity in online business education courses. *Journal of Business and Educational Leadership, 4*(1), 102–112.

University Business. (2012). From lecture capture to remote proctoring: Athens State increases student flexibility. September. *Academic OneFile.* Retrieved from http://go.galegroup.com.ezproxy.tntech.edu/ps/dispBasicSearch.do?prodId=AONE&userGroupName=tel_a_ttul

Watson, G., & Sottile, J. (2010). Cheating in the digital age: Do student cheat more in online courses? *Online Journal of Distance Learning Administration, 13*(1). Retrieved from http://www.westga.edu/~distance/ojdla/spring131/watson131.html

Watters, M. P., Robertson, P. J., & Clark, R. K. (2011). Student perceptions of cheating in online business courses. *Journal of Instructional Pedagogies, 6*, 1–14.

APPENDIX

Remote Proctor Vendor Overview

Remote Proctor Product	Remote Proctor NOW	ProctorU	Kryterion
Vendor	Software Secure, Inc.	ProctorU, Inc.	Kryterion
Phone	(617)-340-6381	(855)-772-8678	(602)-659-4660
Website	www.softwaresecure.com	www.proctoru.com	www.kryteriononline.com
School billing option	Y	Y	Y
Cost to school	Negotiated	Negotiated	Negotiated
Student billing option	Y	Y	Y
Cost to student	$15 per exam	$14.50/1 hour–$21.50/2 hours	$15–$38 per exam
Feedback within 24 hours	N	Y	Y
Feedback – 5 days or less	Y	Y	Y
Live proctor included	N	Y	Y
View screenshots option	Y	Y	Y
View video option	Y	Y	Y
Webcam required	Y	Y	Y
Audio recording	Y	Y	Y
Photo ID authentication	Y	Y	Y
Additional ID authentication	Y	Y[a]	Y[b]
Access through LMS option	Y	Y	Y
Test delivery system option	N	Y	Y[c]
Complimentary practice exam	Y	N	Y
Equipment testing	Y	Y	Y
Lockdown built-in or required	Y	N	Y
Fully takes over student computer	N	N	Y
24/7 support	Y	Y	N

(*Continued*)

Remote Proctor Vendor Overview

Remote Proctor Product	Remote Proctor NOW	ProctorU	Kryterion
Vendor	Software Secure, Inc.	ProctorU, Inc.	Kryterion
Phone	(617)-340-6381	(855)-772-8678	(602)-659-4660
Website	www.softwaresecure.com	www.proctoru.com	www.kryterionline.com

Remote Proctor Product	Respondus Monitor	ProctorCam	B Virtual
Vendor	Respondus, Inc.	Proctorcam, Inc.	B Virtual, Inc.
Phone		(877)-837-8127	(888)-418-4230
Website	www.respondus.com	www.proctorcam.com	www.bvirtualinc.com/
School billing option	Y	Y	Y
Cost to school	$3,950/first 1,000	Negotiated	Negotiated
Student billing option	Y	Y	Y
Cost to student	$10 per semester	$6–$25 per exam[d]	$25/2 hours
Feedback within 24 hours	Y[e]	Y	N
Feedback – 5 days or less	Y	Y	Y
Live proctor included	N	Y[f]	Y
View screenshots option	Y	Y	Y
View video option	Y	Y	Y
Webcam required	N	Y	Y
Audio recording	Y	Y	Y
Photo ID Authentication	N	Y	Y
Additional ID authentication	N	N	Y[g]
Access through LMS option	Y	Y	Y

(Continued)

Remote Proctor Product	Respondus Monitor	ProctorCam	B Virtual
Vendor	Respondus, Inc.	Proctorcam, Inc.	B Virtual, Inc.
Phone		(877)-837-8127	(888)-418-4230
Website	www.respondus.com	www.proctorcam.com	www.bvirtualinc.com/
Test delivery system option	N	N	N
Complimentary practice exam	N[h]	Y	N
Equipment testing	Y	Y	Y
Lockdown built-in or required	Y	N[i]	N
Fully takes over student computer	N		Y
24/7 support	N	Y	Y

Notes: All Information obtained from respective company website, phone calls, live chats, and emails. Information Current through April 14, 2015.

[a] A series of security questioned is asked by live proctor after photo ID is verified.

[b] Facial recognition and keystroke pattern recognition included.

[c] Advanced test delivery system called Webassessor for use in lieu of LMS.

[d] Price varies based on whether live proctor option is elected or not.

[e] Alerts sent to students when questionable activity is detected.

[f] Non-live-proctor option available as well.

[g] Randomized background questions asked by live proctor. Additional layers of authentication included as mandated by institution.

[h] Free Pilot program optional before commitment.

[i] Accessible through mobile devices as an easy-to-use application.

TEACHING VARIANCE ANALYSIS FOR COST ACCOUNTING: HOW TO ACHIEVE ABOVE PAR PERFORMANCE

Ron Messer

ABSTRACT

Purpose − *The tool described is most appropriate for a first-level under-graduate course in cost/management accounting, which is typically taken in the second year of a post-secondary business program.*

Methodology/approach − *This chapter discusses a method for teaching a challenging topic within cost/management accounting, which is calculating variances for expenses. The proposed methodology focuses on a "common sense" understanding of variances as differences between bud-geted and actual results. The new approach (i) uses a golfing analogy as a frame of reference, (ii) includes questions to assist in the analysis, and (iii) provides a table to organize and calculate variances. The variances examined include eight common expense-side variances used by manufac-turers: material price and efficiency variances; labor price and efficiency variances; variable overhead spending and efficiency variances and fixed overhead spending and production volume variances.*

Advances in Accounting Education: Teaching and Curriculum Innovations, Volume 18, 51−63
Copyright © 2016 by Emerald Group Publishing Limited
ISSN: 1085-4622/doi:10.1108/S1085-462220160000018003

Findings — *By using this tool, students will be able to understand how and why variances are calculated. It will also provide them with better insight into appropriate corrective action that will address deviation from plans.*

Originality/value — *I provide a template to facilitate the calculation of variances, along with a list of questions that will guide students in their analysis. I also give an application of the suggested approach, using a standard textbook problem.*

Keywords: Variance analysis; cost accounting; standard costs; budgets; responsibility accounting

I have been teaching an introductory cost accounting course at the post-secondary level for more than 10 years. During this time, I have found the topic that most challenges students about this first-level class is variance analysis.[1] This includes calculating the eight standard "expense-side" variances used by most manufacturing companies, including:

- materials price and efficiency variances,
- labor price and efficiency variances,
- variable overhead spending and efficiency variances,
- fixed overhead spending and production volume variances.

Material and labor price variances relate to the difference between what a company expected to pay for production inputs and what it actually paid. Efficiency variances relate to the quantities of labor and materials used to produce a certain amount of output. Overhead variances (both variable and fixed) address the differences between the indirect costs that are expected to be incurred and what was actually spent, as well as the quantity of the cost driver (e.g., labor hours) used to allocate the overhead costs to production.

Textbooks in cost accounting typically present this topic using two approaches.[2] The first method employs a table format (horizontal approach) to show the type of costs that need to be compared when determining the variances, including actual and standard costs and actual and standard usage. Fig. 1 illustrates this table format.

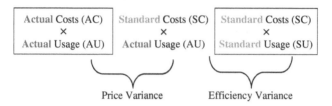

Fig. 1. A Format for Calculating Variances.

The second approach uses formulas to calculate the variances. For example, price variances are the difference between the actual cost (AC) and standard cost (SC) for materials, labor, or overhead, which is then monetized by multiplying the difference by the actual usage (AU) of material, labor, or overhead (cost driver). As a formula, this can be expressed as:

$$(AC - SC) \times AU = Price\,Variance$$

My experience has shown that students will try to learn this material by memorizing the format of either the table or the formulas. Unfortunately, they seldom understand what they are calculating and frequently confuse, or forget the variables in the formulas. This becomes apparent when I ask them to interpret the variances and recommend appropriate corrective action.

LITERATURE REVIEW

Prior research on teaching variance analysis has focused on ways to simplify the calculation/explanation of the differences between budgeted and actual amounts. This has been done by using a variety of substitutes/enhancements for the "numbers" traditionally calculated as part of this exercise, including graphical–visual explanations, non-numeric reasoning, vertical versus horizontal analysis, and contextual re-framing.

In their research, Martin and Laughlin (1988) utilized a visual methodology. Through a series of overlapping transparencies, they developed a logical progression to explain variances which they then graphically illustrated. Shank and Churchill (1977) used a multi-layered analytical approach that focused on understanding the impact of variances on corporate profits. By examining these different "layers," additional insights into the nature of the variances could be obtained. Silvester and O'Neill (2013) utilized cost flow diagrams. While this study did not specifically focus on variance analysis, similar to Martin and Laughlin (1988), the authors discussed the efficacy of using a graphical approach to understanding cost accounting concepts.

Chow (1988) developed a "common sense" approach to analyzing variances that was not based on formulas. It also reconciled the non-formula approach with the calculations traditionally performed and explained how the two methods were mutually re-enforcing.

Smith (1991) created a "vertical" method for analyzing variances (in contrast to the more traditional horizontal approach – see Fig. 1) that integrated fixed and variable overhead into a simple formula. Little and Saubert (1997) provided a further elaboration of a vertical analysis for overhead variances, using a highly structured approach.

Spraakman and Jackling (2014) considered the use of a different conceptual framework to teach cost accounting that focused on developing students' problem-solving abilities rather than having them simply memorize definitions and explanations. VanZante (2007) advocated the use of case studies to better illustrate how variances are calculated, demonstrating the equivalencies of several different methods used for this purpose.

While the use of analogies for teaching variance analysis (such as golf) has not been explored in the context of cost accounting, Martin (2003) has discussed their use in teaching an introductory statistics course, finding that analogies are effective when communicating complex ideas to students.

A NEW APPROACH

Initially, when I began teaching variance analysis, I followed the two approaches used by most textbook authors. I realized, however, when evaluating students' responses to exam questions on this topic that they were merely mimicking solutions covered in class, as evidenced by their poor test scores. For this reason, I began to think about alternative ways to teach variance analysis. To do this, I considered the topic in a more conceptual way.[3]

At its most basic level, a variance is simply a difference between two things that can be quantified. It is therefore important to identify the things that need to be compared. At this point, I began to consider a golfing analogy. Keeping score in golf can be done either by counting the number of strokes (i.e., golf swings) in a game or by tracking the difference between the strokes taken and par for each hole. Par is like a standard. The number of shots taken is similar to the actual costs/quantities incurred by a manufacturer. A bogey can be considered to be an unfavorable variance; birdies and eagles are favorable variances.

In conjunction with the traditional approach to teaching this topic, I introduced what I called the "common sense" way of doing variance analysis (which is different from the approach suggested by Chow, 1988, because of its use of an analogy and directed enquiry). To me, analyzing variances was about asking questions concerning why things didn't go according to plan. There will always be differences between what we thought was going to happen and what actually occurs (remember how great a golfer you considered yourself to be until you counted your score). Variances provide us with a means of not only quantifying this difference but also gaining insight into how it happened.

Instructors typically tell students that there are eight standard expense-side variances; however, I contend that there are essentially just two general types of differences that need to be examined and explained: (1) cost variances (which are measured in dollars) and (2) usage variances (which are measured as a quantity – e.g., kilograms of coal; meters of material; hours of labor time). I tell students to consider keeping score in a different way. Rather than thinking about variance analysis as a number crunching exercise, scorekeeping should be based on an analysis of differences, like the difference from par for each hole in a golf game. This involves the following steps:

1. *identifying* and *comparing* relevant data,
2. asking appropriate questions about the differences that are identified, and
3. *calculating* the dollar impact of the differences.

Step 1: Identify and Compare the Relevant Data – Keeping Score

In order to more clearly elucidate the concept of variances, I ask students, after reading the case facts for a practice exercise, to do the following.

1. Identify the *standard cost* and *usage* for material, labor, and overhead – what's par for the course?
2. Identify the *actual cost* and *usage* for material, labor, and overhead – what was the actual number of strokes?
3. Compare *actual* and *standard costs* and *usage* for material, labor, and overhead – was the hole (i.e., cost or usage) a bogey or a birdie (favorable or unfavorable variance)?

Step 2: Understand What Happened by Asking Questions — Bogey or Birdie

After identifying and comparing relevant data, I ask the following questions and invite discussion:[4]

- How much was paid for each unit of material, labor, or overhead?
- Was this more or less than expected (i.e., compared to the standard or budget)?
- How much of each unit of material, labor, or overhead was used to produce a unit of output?
- Was this more or less than expected (i.e., compared to the standard or budget)?

I then enquire about the impact of these differences and who is responsible for them? The intent is to link the variances calculated to the notion of responsibility accounting and budget management.

- If we paid more, or used more, for our materials, labor, and other inputs, who should be held accountable for this (and why)?
- How can we determine whether a variance is significant? (Students should realize that there will always be a difference between planned and actual results, with the probability of them being the same extremely low.)
- Finally, if corrective action is required, what can we do to rectify the variance?

At this point, students begin to understand the reason for performing variance analysis. They realize that it is not just to calculate a number, but rather to gain insight into a problem — the problem of whether or not expectations have been met. Expectations are tied to plans, which in turn permit management control. Variance analysis is an important management tool that can be used to improve a company's performance. In this way, variances become linked to the notion of responsibility accounting, which means holding someone accountable for corporate objectives, including consequences for both success and failure. It is critical that students realize that variance analysis is fundamentally a tool that facilitates decision making and leads to better management. It provides useful information for companies and is linked to other accounting concepts, such as standard costing, principal/agent relations (goal congruency), and corporate strategy.

Step 3: Calculate the Variances for Decision Making — Improving Your Game

Once students have identified the relevant data concerning actual and standard costs and usage, and they have completed a discussion about the reason for the differences, they can use Table 1 to conveniently calculate (quantify) the variances.

It is important to note that students should only use this table *after* they have completed the conceptual exercise of identifying data and asking appropriate questions. The table is intended to summarize and quantify the differences analyzed and should never be a substitute for genuine understanding. All three components are linked and should be done sequentially.

Actual cost/usage of materials, labor, and overhead — based on a unit of output — will be provided in the problem case facts, or may have to be calculated. Variable/fixed overhead cost/usage per unit will be based on the cost driver used to allocate indirect costs. Standard (or budgeted) cost/usage amounts are generally presented on the same basis as actual cost/usage.

Cost variances for materials are based on the quantity *purchased*, whereas efficiency variances are based on the actual *usage* of materials during production. Because labor is not inventoried, the cost and usage variances are both based on the units produced.

If the actual amount exceeds the standard, then the variance is unfavorable (otherwise, it is favorable), as cost or usage was greater than expected, resulting in additional dollars being spent and therefore lowering income.

Once the students have calculated variances, they should not have difficulty preparing journal entries, as we will have covered this topic in previous classes. The quantified variances represent an extension of the discussion about recording transactions in a cost accounting system and are highlighted in the new ledger accounts that are created to show favorable or unfavorable results.

AN APPLICATION OF THE METHOD

A furniture manufacturer produces 7,800 units of output, with the following cost structure. (*Note*: hrs.= direct labor hours. U = Unfavorable variance; F = Favorable variance.)

In this example, "par" for the course is represented by the standard cost and usage amounts. The differences between standard and actual results

Table 1. Input Variables Used for Calculating and Analyzing Variances.

Item	Identify[a] Actual	Identify Standard	Compare Actual vs. Standard	Calculate
Input and unit of measure (e.g., cost per unit)	Cost per input unit or usage per output unit	Cost per input unit or usage per output unit	Difference in cost per input unit or usage per output unit	*Cost variances:* Multiply actual versus standard difference by *actual* quantity purchased (materials) or used (labor hours or O/H cost driver)
				Usage variances: Multiply actual versus standard difference by *standard* cost and actual production

Direct material (e.g., $ per kg)
  Cost variance
  Usage variance
Direct labor (e.g., $ per labor hour)
  Cost variance
  Usage variance
Variable overhead (e.g., $ per machine hour)
  Cost variance
  Usage variance
Fixed overhead (e.g., $ per machine hour)
  Cost variance
  Usage variance[b] (production volume variance)

[a] A cost comparison is used to identify *price* variances; usage comparisons identify *efficiency* variances. Sometimes cost variances are referred to as "rate" or "spending" variances. Note that there is no efficiency variance for fixed overhead; instead, a production volume variance is calculated.

[b] The production volume variance, unlike usage variances for materials, labor, and variable overhead, compares the planned and the standard activity level for the cost driver.

are either favorable (birdie) or unfavorable outcomes (bogey). Making enquiries about those who have primary responsibility for purchasing (material price variance), labor rates (labor price variance), and production (efficiency variances) will help determine appropriate corrective action (Table 2).

I began using this approach in the winter term of my third calendar year of teaching variance analysis. Over the subsequent period, it was my impression that students' performance was improving and that they understood the topic better using my new teaching method. I based this preliminary conclusion on the quality of the classroom discussion on variance analysis, as well as students' performance on examinations. However, it was not until I analyzed the data that it became apparent that improvement had, in fact, occurred.

THE RESULTS

At the institution where I teach, it is a common practice to administer standardized examinations. This allows for better comparison of student performance across various classes and different instructors. It also allowed me to track students' understanding of variance analysis, as the format of this question on the final exam remained relatively unchanged over time, with only occasional revisions to some of the numbers used to calculate cost and usage variances. The question specifically asked students to: (i) calculate the eight "expense-side" variances, (ii) provide a plausible explanation for their occurrence, and then (iii) prepare the appropriate journal entries to record the variances in the accounting system (i.e., journalize and post the transactions to the general ledger). About 25 marks, or one quarter of the total available marks on the exam, were awarded for this question.

In total, approximately 300 students answered this problem over a period of 15 academic terms, or 5 calendar years. Students' performance improved significantly in the winter term of year 3, which was the time that I introduced my "common sense" method of teaching variance analysis. Those receiving a passing grade (typically 60% or better, which is required by most university accounting programs) improved from approximately 30−60% of students writing this question.

The graph in Fig. 2 shows that the average (mean) and median mark for the variance analysis question, indicating an improvement in the scores for

Table 2. A Numerical Application of the Method.[a]

Cost/Usage Element	Actual	Standard
Direct material	25,000 kg bought @$5.20/kg; 23,100 kg used to make 7,800 units	3 kg/unit @ $5/kg
Direct labor	40,100 hrs. used to make 7,800 units @ $14.60/hr.	5 hrs./unit @ $15/hr.
Variable overhead	$250,000; 40,100 hrs. used	$6/hr. assuming 40,000 hrs.
Fixed overhead	$350,000; 7,800 × 5 = 39,000 hrs. allocated	$8/hr. assuming 40,000 hrs.

Item	Identify[a] Actual	Identify Standard	Compare Actual vs. Standard	Calculate
Input and unit of measure (e.g., cost per unit)	Cost per input unit or usage per output unit	Cost per input unit or usage per output unit	Difference in cost per input unit or usage per output unit	*Cost variances:* Multiply actual versus standard difference by *actual* quantity purchased (materials) or used (labor hours or O/H cost driver)
				Usage variances: **Multiply actual versus standard difference by *standard* cost and actual production**
Direct material				
Cost variance	$5.20/kg	$5.00/kg	$0.20/kg	$0.20 × 25,000 = $5,000U
Usage variance	2.96 kg/unit[b]	3 kg/unit	0.0385kg/unit	0.0385 × 7,800 × $5 = $1,500F
Direct labor				
Cost variance	$14.60/hr.	$15.00/hr.	$0.40/hr.	$0.40 × 40,100 = 16,040F
Usage variance	5.14 hrs./unit[b]	5 hrs./unit	0.14 hrs./unit	0.14[a] × 7800 × $15 = 16,500U
Variable overhead				
Cost variance	$6.23/hr.[b]	$6.00/hr.	$0.23/hr.	0.23 × 40,100 = $9,400U
Usage variance	5.14 hrs./unit[b]	5 hrs./unit	0.14 hrs./unit	0.14[a] × 7,800 × $6 = 6,600U
Fixed overhead				
Cost variance[b]	$8.75/hr.[b]	$8.00/hr.	0.75/hr.	0.75 × 40,000 = $30,000U
Usage variance[b] (production volume variance)	$8.21/hr.[b]	$8.00/hr.	0.21/hr.	0.21 × 39,000 = $8,000U

[a]*Source:* The case facts for this application exercise have been excerpted from the well-known text by Charles Horngren: *Cost Accounting: A Management Emphasis.* See Problem 8–40 from the 6th Canadian edition. Some modification has been made to the case facts to show separate amounts for the actual variable and fixed overhead amounts.

[b]Numbers have been rounded and therefore the variance calculations may not be exact (23,100/7,800 = 2.96; 40,000/7,800 = 5.14; 250,000/40,100 = 6.23; 350,000/40,000 = 8.75; 320,000/39,000 = 8.21).

this topic area from 53% to 68% for the average grade and from 52% to 73% for the median grade.

LIMITATIONS OF STUDY

Class sizes for this study varied from 15 to 25 students. Even though some classes were small, we can still make preliminary observations about the efficacy of the new teaching method. Over the nine terms that the new method was used, grades varied (as shown in Fig. 2); however, the median mark was consistently better than 60%. The variability in post-implementation scores can be attributed to normally occurring differences in the abilities of students taking this course. While these results may not be conclusive, they do suggest that an approach that focuses on understanding the "differences" between costs being compared (i.e., what's par?) is foundational to helping students comprehend the underlying purpose of variance analysis.

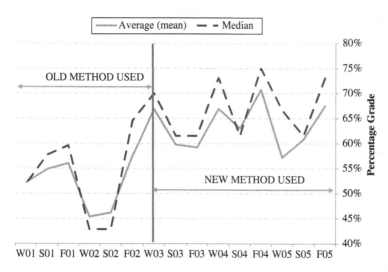

Fig. 2. Student Average and Median Grade for Variance Analysis Question on Final Exam. *Notes:* The horizontal axis descriptions refer to the academic term (S = Spring; W = Winter; F = Fall) and the year of testing (e.g., year 1, year 2, etc.). Therefore, W03 is the winter term of year 3.

CONCLUSIONS

I have always believed that it is more important to understand cost accounting at a conceptual level, rather than simply learning it through rote memorization. However, far too many students enrolled in such a course try to regurgitate formulas, formats, or approaches. This is not the best method for learning this accounting topic, which is primarily an exercise in problem solving. It requires an understanding of the purpose of variance analysis; which is to interpret differences between planned and actual results.

The teaching method suggested in this chapter is used to some extent by other faculty with whom I have had discussions. They have also struggled with providing a more common sense epproach to what experienced partitioners find a relatively simple exercise. But, inevitably — as they have told me and as I have found — students conveniently regress to memorization when comprehension is found to be other than immediate.

Common sense explanations, including using a golfing analogy, have helped to elucidate the subject for many of the students in my classes. Not surprisingly, they have appreciated this type of explanation because it provides both content and context for what is generally perceived as a daunting course in the accounting curriculum. What was once considered a handicap to a student's GPA has become an above par experience.

NOTES

1. The cost accounting course was 13 weeks in duration with the topic of variance analysis covered after the mid-term exam, which was typically during class number eight and nine. I devoted two class sessions (six hours) to the topic. Cost/management accounting is usually taught as three separate courses: introductory, intermediate and advanced (the latter being case-based). Expense-side variance analysis is covered at the introductory level.

2. Charles Horngren's Cost Accounting text (Cost Accounting: A Managerial Emphasis), is a well-known standard course textbook used by many institutions, and was required in my classes.

3. Other approaches to teaching variances in the cost accounting curriculum include more extensive use of case studies. While case analysis can be a very effective tool, it generally requires students to have mastered a certain body of knowledge. This is why cases are taught primarily in graduate programs (e.g., MBA), or in the senior year of an undergraduate program. To date, the teaching method outlined in this chapter has not been discussed with textbook publishers.

4. As a pedagogue, I have always tried to use an enquiry based method of instruction, soliciting input from students about the topics covered in class and asking them to challenge the underlying assumptions.

REFERENCES

Chow, C. W. (1988). A common sense approach to teaching variance analysis. *The Accounting Educator's Journal, Spring*, 42–48.

Little, P., & Saubert, L. K. (1997). An alternative vertical approach to analyzing overhead variances. *Academy of Accounting and Financial Studies Journal, 1*(1), 61–67.

Martin, J. R., & Laughlin, E. J. (1988). A graphic approach to variance analysis emphasizes concepts rather than mechanics. *Issues in Accounting Education, Fall*, 351–364.

Martin, M. A. (2003). "It's like ... you know": The use of analogies and heuristics in teaching introductory statistical methods. *Journal of Statistics Education, 11*(2). Retrieved from http://www.amstat.org/publications/jse/v11n2/martin.html

Shank, J. K., & Churchill, N. C. (1977). Variance analysis: A management oriented approach. *The Accounting Review, 52*(4), 950–957.

Silvester, K. J., & O'Neill, J. C. (2013, July). *Cost flow diagrams as an alternative method of external representation*. Working Paper. Siena College.

Smith, K. J. (1991). An alternative method of variance analysis instruction. *The Accounting Educator's Journal, Winter*, 75–94.

Spraakman, G., & Jackling, B. (2014). A Conceptual Framework for Learning Management Accounting. *Accounting Perspectives, 13*(1), 61–81. doi: 10.1111/1911-3838.12024

VanZante, N. R. (2007). Helping students see the big picture on variance analysis. *Management Accounting Quarterly, Spring*, 39–47.

SPECIAL SECTION ON ACCOUNTING DOCTORAL PROGRAMS AND THE ACADEMIC JOB MARKET

INTRODUCTION TO SPECIAL SECTION ON ACCOUNTING: DOCTORAL PROGRAMS AND THE ACADEMIC JOB MARKET

In this special section, we include three chapters that address important issues related to doctoral programs. For those who are considering entering a doctoral program, a key decision is choosing a doctoral program that fits with the candidate's long-term goals. In the first chapter of this special section, Brink and Quick provide a guide to some of the key factors that those who are planning to enter an accounting doctoral program should consider. Surveying current doctoral students from 60 different programs in the United States, the authors compare programs on a variety of dimensions, including curriculum, research support, and teaching expectations. The information they've gathered should prove valuable to anyone considering entering an accounting doctoral program as well as any faculty member who is approached by students seeking advice about entering an accounting doctoral program.

In the second chapter, Abdullah, Brink, Eller, and Gouldman examine a key aspect of the doctoral student experience that often receives minimal attention − teaching experience. These researchers survey doctoral students from accounting as well as several related disciplines (including management, finance, and economics) to provide a picture of the pedagogical training that doctoral students receive in the various disciplines. They find that accounting and management doctoral students feel better prepared to teach undergraduate courses than students from other disciplines, but students from all disciplines feel inadequately prepared to teach graduate classes as they prepare to begin their career as a faculty member. The authors suggest opportunities for doctoral programs that wish to incorporate pedagogical training for their students.

Finally, the third chapter by Bergner, Filzen, and Wong offers advice for those doctoral students who are completing their doctoral studies and are planning to enter the academic job market. In recent years, the academic job market for accounting doctoral students has seen considerable change (especially the introduction of the Rookie Camp developed by the University of Miami). The authors of this third chapter draw on their own experiences as well as interviews with recent participants in the job market to provide advice and guidance for those who plan to enter this market. We hope that this information serves as a helpful supplement to the advice and guidance that doctoral students are receiving from the faculty mentors in their respective programs.

Beth B. Kern
Timothy J. Rupert
Co-editors

ACCOUNTING DOCTORAL PROGRAM CHARACTERISTICS: A GUIDE FOR PROSPECTIVE STUDENTS

William D. Brink and Linda A. Quick

ABSTRACT

Purpose — *To provide potential accounting doctoral students with relevant information on various doctoral program characteristics.*

Methodology/approach — *Current doctoral students in accounting, representing 60 different programs in the United States, completed a survey concerning various doctoral program characteristics at their respective doctoral institutions. We examine the survey responses along with program rankings and job placement data.*

Findings — *Doctoral programs in accounting differ on many dimensions such as the structure of the courses and deliverables required, the student cohort profile, student research support, and teaching expectations. In addition, top tier programs differ on a variety of these characteristics from lower tiered programs.*

Research limitations/implications — *A single student at each doctoral program completed the survey. Doctoral students' experiences may differ*

Advances in Accounting Education: Teaching and Curriculum Innovations, Volume 18, 69–109

Copyright © 2016 by Emerald Group Publishing Limited

All rights of reproduction in any form reserved

ISSN: 1085-4622/doi:10.1108/S1085-462220160000018004

between each other and programs may change. However, we asked students to respond to the survey questions as a "typical student" and as a whole, doctoral programs appear to have remained similar over the past half of century.

Originality/value — *The intended audience for this chapter is potential accounting doctoral students. Providing them with an awareness of the different program characteristics should prove to be useful in finding a program with the appropriate fit.*

Keywords: Accounting Ph.D.; accounting doctoral programs; doctoral education

There is a shortage of accounting faculty at higher education institutions (Behn, Carnes, Krull, Stocks, & Reckers, 2008; Plumlee, Kachelmeier, Madeo, Pratt, and Krull, 2006; Urbancic, 2008). As a result, various programs have been created to help stimulate interest in doctoral programs in accounting. For example, over 65 accounting firms and over 48 state CPA societies developed the Accounting Doctoral Scholars Program (ADS) to fund potential doctoral students.[1] Despite the push to encourage more potential students to pursue a doctoral degree in accounting, it is often difficult to obtain the information needed to decide not only *whether* a doctoral degree is the right fit for a particular person, but also *which* doctoral program may be the best fit.

The primary purpose of this chapter is to provide potential doctoral students relevant information on various doctoral program characteristics. An accounting doctoral program generally has two stages: the coursework stage and the dissertation preparation stage. Although most all doctoral programs in the United States utilize this two-stage design, every program is unique. Doctoral programs in accounting differ on many dimensions such as the structure of the courses and deliverables required, the student cohort profile, student research support, and teaching expectations. Potential doctoral students' awareness of these differences should prove to be useful in finding a doctoral program with the appropriate fit. We obtained survey responses from current doctoral students in accounting, representing 60 of the 95 different programs in the United States. In this chapter, we present our survey results in the form of addressing common questions a potential doctoral student may want to consider. We present a list of potential questions in Fig. 1.

In addition to providing the descriptive information from the survey responses, we make several observations of the pros and cons of the various characteristics. We base these observations primarily on the experiences of the authors and conversations with various colleagues. The intent of this chapter is not to guide potential students to pursue a doctoral degree at a particular institution, but instead to enlighten potential students on how various programs may differ so that they can find the institution that best aligns with their goals.

The next section of this chapter briefly discusses some of the previous literature regarding accounting doctoral programs and careers. Next, we discuss the survey research methodology used to collect data for this chapter. We discuss and present survey results as follows: first, we present a section discussing doctoral courses and deliverables, followed by a section discussing student cohorts. The third section of results discusses student research support, followed by a section discussing the student teaching expectations. The final section of this chapter offers conclusions and some additional insights for prospective doctoral students to consider.

ADDITIONAL USEFUL READINGS

In addition to this chapter, there are three other papers that may prove to be useful for potential accounting doctoral students. First, Beyer, Herrmann, Meek, and Rapley (2010) wrote an article titled "What it means to be an Accounting Professor: A Concise Career Guide for Doctoral Students in Accounting." Second, Hermanson (2008) wrote an article titled "What I Have Learned So Far: Observations on Managing an Academic Accounting Career." Both of these papers are useful guides in helping doctoral students select employment at an institution of fit *after obtaining* their accounting doctoral degree. The third paper, Bergner (2009), "Pursuing a Ph.D. in Accounting: Walking in With your Eyes Open," is a commentary on one doctoral student's experiences at the University of Kentucky.

One of the most important decisions an accounting faculty will make is what doctoral program to attend. This chapter adds to the prior papers by discussing the various characteristics of doctoral programs in general, rather than focusing on employment selection post-doctoral degree or a single doctoral program. In doing so, this chapter should be a useful guide to help potential doctoral students understand how these programs may differ and allow them to make a more informed decision on which accounting doctoral program to attend.

Other papers in the accounting literature have addressed issues related to ranking accounting doctoral programs (McGee, 1999; Urbancic, 2008); and foreign students obtaining terminal degrees in accounting in the United States (Cho, Roberts, & Roberts, 2008). However, no study, to our knowledge, has looked at a comprehensive set of characteristics of accounting doctoral programs. Imhoff (1988) offers some descriptive evidence on doctoral programs; however, the focus of this chapter is mainly on how the programs could be designed to maximize the benefits for the existing skill sets of incoming doctoral students, rather than discussing details on how accounting doctoral programs are currently designed. As such, we hope that our study will fill a void in the current literature by providing helpful information on program characteristics to prospective doctoral students.

Behn et al. (2008) survey accounting doctoral program coordinators, asking questions about factors that influence which students are accepted into a doctoral program (e.g., average GMAT scores), areas of research, and research methods of the universities' doctoral students. Our study focuses on a different set of doctoral program characteristics, not documented within the accounting literature, such as the number and type of seminars taken, and the number and type of courses taught. While previous studies have focused on ranking accounting doctoral programs based on quality (Urbancic, 2008) or suggesting ways in which programs might be improved (McGee, 1999), our chapter is not meant to provide a ranking or comment on the quality of the programs, but rather to offer descriptive evidence regarding the characteristics of accounting doctoral programs.

RESEARCH METHODOLOGY

This chapter seeks to provide potential doctoral students with relevant information regarding accounting doctoral programs in the United States. There are multiple ways to collect this information. Doctoral program

What are the **course requirements** for graduation?
    How many accounting seminars will I be expected to take?
    How are the accounting seminars structured (e.g., research methodology or subject matter)?
    What are the accounting seminars I will be expected to take?
    In which departments outside of accounting will I be expected to take elective courses?
What are the **other requirements** for graduation?
    How many research papers will I be expected to write?
    Is there a comprehensive examination?
    If so, how is the comprehensive exam structured?
What will my **student cohort** look like?
    How often are new students admitted?
    How many new students are admitted?
    How many students are currently in the doctoral program?
    How long will it take for me to graduate?
    What is the percent of students who start the program and eventually graduate?
What kind of **research support** does the program offer?
    Does your program fund/support research conference travel?
    What type of professor will I be working with?
    Will I be assigned as a research assistant?
What are the **teaching expectations** for the program?
    How many different courses will I be expected to teach?
    How many times will I be expected to teach each course?
    What level(s) of course(s) will I be expected to teach?

Fig. 1. Potential Questions for Prospective Doctoral Students to Consider. *Note*: This list of potential questions for prospective doctoral students to consider is not an exhaustive list. For example, other factors that should be considered by potential doctoral students is the program's reputation, student placements after graduation, reputation of the current faculty, student stipend amounts, and even geographic location.

characteristics can be obtained from the program coordinators, former students, current students, and from each institution's respective website to name a few. Each of these information sources has pros and cons.

Doctoral program coordinators are often in charge of the doctoral students. They are a good source of information; however, their perspective of what is expected of students may differ from a student's perspective. In addition, at some point in a doctoral student's education, the student will work more closely with an advisor, which is likely different than the doctoral program coordinator. This may lead to the program coordinator being more distant from the student experience. For prospective students, it may be most useful to obtain information from current students as they have the most recent experience with their program. Therefore, we obtained the data for this survey from students enrolled in a doctoral program in the United States at the time they took the survey (during the 2013/2014 academic year).

Obtaining survey data from current students also has drawbacks. Specifically, just as program characteristics differ based on the institution, each individual student's experience can be different. Despite this drawback, current students have an up close and personal experience with their respective doctoral programs and are the best source of information based on the goals of this chapter. To help eliminate some of the personal biases that can occur when responding to the survey, we asked students to answer the survey questions as they pertain to a "typical student" in their respective doctoral program. The survey instrument, showing the exact wording of questions asked, is located in Appendix A.

We present the results of this study in aggregate, rather than providing detailed responses for each institution. This format was necessary to hold specific doctoral student responses anonymous; however, it does not interfere with the goal of this chapter, which is to provide prospective doctoral students with information on the different types of doctoral programs. Once prospective doctoral students have an understanding of the various characteristics of a doctoral program, they should obtain additional information about specific institutions.

The Hasselback Accounting Faculty Directory (2012) lists the academic institutions that have granted doctoral degrees in accounting. We identified a current doctoral student from each of these institutions and asked them to participate in an online survey about their respective doctoral program.[2] We received 60 student responses representing approximately 63% of the doctoral programs in accounting in the United States. Table 1 contains a list of doctoral programs, and we designate those represented in our survey with boldface type. The median (mean) year of residency of the current students participating in this study was 4 (4.06), suggesting that our respondents should be very familiar with their respective programs.[3]

SURVEY RESULTS

Our intention is that the results from this survey will provide prospective doctoral students with an understanding of how doctoral programs in accounting can vary and on what dimensions. We present the results in aggregate form and we do not describe individual doctoral program characteristic details. However, in addition to providing information in aggregate, we also present any significant differences between doctoral program characteristics based on the program's tier.[4]

To categorize doctoral programs into three equal tiers, this chapter uses the "Accounting Research Rankings: Accounting Ph.D. Rankings 2014" developed by Brigham Young University. These rankings rank doctoral programs based on the research output of the graduates of the program, based on the number of publications in 11 accounting journals. Table 1 shows the accounting doctoral programs in each tier. Understanding differences between how tier 1 doctoral programs and tier 2 or tier 3 doctoral programs are designed will be useful for prospective doctoral students.

Courses and Deliverables

How Many Accounting Courses Should I Expect at Your Program?

Doctoral students typically have a "program of study," which outlines the required courses that they must take in order to obtain a doctoral degree in accounting. The program of study generally has at least two categories. The first category is the accounting doctoral courses/seminars that are required and the second category is a list of possible elective courses. Institutions offering a doctoral degree in accounting often differ greatly on the number of accounting courses it requires their doctoral students to complete in order to obtain a terminal degree in accounting.

Responses from the survey indicate that the median (mean) number of accounting seminars required for a terminal degree in accounting was 4 (4.72). This is consistent with McGee (1999), who looked at five different doctoral curriculums, each of which had four required accounting seminars. Although 58.33% of the participants indicated that their respective program had either four or five required accounting seminars, the range was significant with a low of one seminar to a high of 10 seminars. Although one accounting seminar seems quite low and 10 seminars seem quite high, after reviewing the institutions' specific doctoral websites, it appears that there is not a clear delineation between what constitutes an accounting seminar. For example, some schools offer independent studies, which can be considered accounting seminars. Fig. 2 Panel A presents the frequencies of the number of accounting courses offered through the accounting department for the institutions included in the survey.

The number of accounting seminars could impact a prospective student's decision to attend a specific institution for a number of reasons. One specific benefit of taking a greater number of accounting seminars is that it introduces students to a much broader application of accounting research. Once a doctoral student obtains employment after graduation, he/she will likely narrow the focus of their research stream. Therefore, the doctoral program may be the best opportunity to gain an understanding of the many facets of accounting research.

Another benefit of taking a greater number of accounting courses is that it introduces the doctoral students to the accounting faculty on a professional and personal level. Accounting seminars are often very intimate with only two to eight students per course. This small course size allows the respective professor and the students to have significant interactions. It is very important to develop positive working relationships with multiple faculty members, and more seminars offered allows for this opportunity. In fact, based on our survey results, there appears to be a very strong relationship between the number of accounting seminars required and having a primary mentor that is a full professor.[5]

There are also drawbacks to attending an institution requiring a greater number of accounting seminars. First, the number of courses in total is often fixed. That is, the more accounting seminars a student takes, the less electives the student will be allowed to take outside the accounting department. If a student is interested in a more broad education, including significant understanding of the research performed in other disciplines, they may benefit from attending an institution with a lower number of required accounting seminars. Another possible drawback to attending an institution requiring a greater number of required courses is that it may detract from a student's ability to focus on a dissertation topic. When completing a dissertation in a specific field, doctoral students are expected to completely immerse themselves into that field. If a student is still taking courses, this immersion into a specific field may be difficult and delayed.

How Are the Accounting Courses Structured at Your Institution?

In addition to the number of accounting seminars required in a doctoral program, it is also important to consider how the structure of accounting seminars can differ between universities. For example, some universities have a methodological focus in their seminars, while other universities separate their seminars based on subject matter. Behn et al. (2008) discuss that accounting research can be classified into six broad subjects (financial accounting and reporting, management accounting, auditing, taxation, information systems, and other). The "other" category includes things like international accounting and accounting education. Behn et al. (2008) also

Table 1. Accounting Doctoral Programs in the United States.[a]

Tier 1	Tier 2	Tier 3
Arizona State University	**Boston University**	**Baruch College**
Carnegie Mellon University	Case Western University	**Bentley University**
Chicago University	Drexel University	Binghamton University
Columbia University	Duke University	**Florida Atlantic University**
Cornell University	**Emory University**	George Washington University
Harvard University	Florida International University	**Jackson State University**
Kansas University	**Florida State University**	**Louisiana State University**
Massachusetts Institute of Technology	**Georgia Institute of Technology**	Louisiana Tech University
Michigan State University	**Georgia State University**	Mississippi State University
New York University	Kent State University	Morgan State University
Northwestern University	**Purdue University**	**Oklahoma State University**
Ohio State University	Rutgers University	**Southern Illinois University**
Pennsylvania State University	Syracuse University	Union College
Stanford University	**Texas Tech University**	University at Buffalo
Temple University	**University of Arkansas**	University Cincinnati
Texas A&M University	University of California-Berkeley	University of California – Los Angeles
University of Alabama	**University of Central Florida**	University of California-Irvine
University of Arizona	**University of Colorado**	**University of Connecticut**
University of Georgia	**University of Florida**	University of Hawaii
University of Illinois	**University of Massachusetts**	University of Houston
University of Indiana	**University of Minnesota**	University of Kentucky
University of Iowa	**University of Nebraska**	**University of Maryland**
University of Michigan	**University of Oregon**	**University of Memphis**
University of Missouri	University of Rochester	University of Miami
University of North Carolina	**University of South Carolina**	**University of Mississippi**
University of Pennsylvania	University of South Florida	University of North Texas
University of Pittsburgh	**University of Tennessee**	University of Oklahoma
University of Southern California	**University of Texas-San Antonio**	**University of Texas-Arlington**
University of Texas-Austin	**University of Utah**	University of Texas-El Paso
University of Texas-Dallas	**Virginia Polytechnic Institute and State University**	**Virginia Commonwealth University**
University of Washington	**Washington University in St. Louis**	**Washington State University**
University of Wisconsin	Yale University	

[a]The table is a list of accounting doctoral programs in the United States. This list was obtained from Hasselback Accounting Faculty Directory (Hasselback, 2012). Survey responses were obtained from the 60 institutions above in boldface print. The three tiers were developed using the BYU Accounting Research Rankings: Accounting Ph.D. Rankings 2014 available at: http://www.byuaccounting.net/rankings/phdrank/rank_phd.php?qurank=All&sortorder=ranking66

discuss the four major distinct research methodologies (archival, behavioral, experimental, and analytical). Institutions may organize their accounting seminars by subject area or research methodology, or a combination.

When we asked the students to indicate on an 11-point scale "Are the accounting seminars at your institution methodology-based (e.g., archival, experimental economics, behavioral, etc.) or subject-based (e.g., audit, financial accounting, etc.)?" (1 = Methodology-based and 11 = Subject-based), the median (mean) response was 7 (6.35) with a standard deviation of 3.04, indicating a lot of variability in the responses to this question.[6] Further analysis shows that approximately 26.67% of student responses indicated that their university's seminars were primarily methodology-based by indicating a 1 through 3 on the scale above, while approximately 28.33% of the student participants indicated that their university's seminars were primarily subject-based by indicating a 9 through 11 on the scale above. The other 45% of the students indicated that their accounting seminars were mixed. For example, some of the universities may offer a Financial Accounting and Reporting Seminar and a Behavioral Research Seminar.

There appears to be some significant differences between tier 1, tier 2, and tier 3 programs and the accounting seminars that are offered. For example, overall, 40% of participants identified that their program offered an Audit Seminar. However, doctoral programs in tier 2 are more likely to offer an audit-specific seminar than doctoral programs in tier 1 (52.38% vs. 28%, respectively; p-value = 0.098). Similarly, in total 45% of programs offer a Behavioral Accounting Research Seminar, but it appears that tier 3 programs are more likely to do so than tier 2 programs (64.29% vs. 33.33%, respectively; p-value = 0.076). Further, 10% of programs offer an Experimental Economic Research Seminar, but it appears that tier 3 programs are more likely to do so than tier 2 programs (14.29% vs. 4.76%, respectively; p-value = 0.079). Finally, although overall 35% of programs offer an Analytical Accounting Research Seminar, these seminars are more likely to be in a tier 1 curriculum (52%) than either a tier 2 (23.81%) or tier 3 (21.43%) curriculum (p-value = 0.046 and p-value = 0.055, respectively).

The structure of the accounting seminars is important for prospective students to consider in order to align research interest with the seminar structure. For example, if a prospective student wants to be an expert at archival research, that individual may benefit from attending an institution offering a seminar devoted specifically to archival research. On the other hand, if a prospective student wants to be an expert in audit research, that individual may benefit from attending an institution offering a seminar

Panel A – "How many **seminars** do the Accounting PhD students take at your institution which are **offered through the accounting department**?"

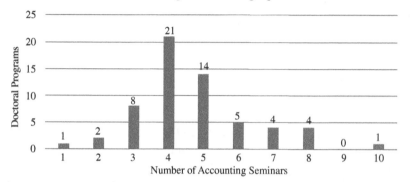

Panel B – "The **accounting seminars** offered at your institution through the accounting department."

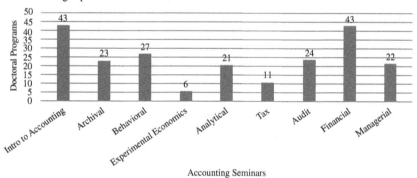

Panel C – "The department from which students typically take core courses and **elective courses** other than accounting seminars."

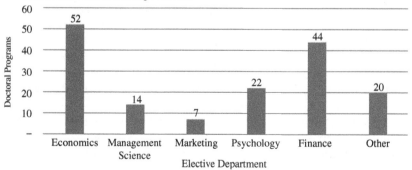

Fig. 2. Course Details.

devoted specifically to audit research. Fig. 2 Panel B offers the frequencies with which specific methodology-based and subject-based seminars are offered at doctoral programs throughout the United States, based on the survey responses. This separation, however, can be somewhat too simplistic. For example, an institution may offer an audit seminar focusing only on papers using a behavioral methodology. It is important to understand the structure of the course offerings from both a research methodology standpoint and subject matter standpoint.

In What Department(s) are Electives Offered at Your Institution?
As stated earlier, a terminal degree in accounting generally involves coursework in the accounting department, plus one or more additional departments. These electives taken in disciplines outside of accounting have an important impact on the development of accounting doctoral students. Prospective students should align their research interests with the courses they will take at their respective universities. Imhoff (1988) explains that a supporting area of coursework will normally influence the nature of the student's research throughout his or her career.

Fig. 2 Panel C reports the frequency of institutions that offer electives in the economics department, the finance department, the psychology department, the management science department, and the marketing department. Although less frequent, multiple students also indicated that their respective universities offer electives in statistics and/or mathematics, sociology, and education. In addition to taking electives in disciplines outside of the accounting department, two of the student participants indicated that they were permitted to take electives at outside universities that could be applied toward their terminal degree in accounting.

It is interesting to note that overall 23.33% of the participants indicated that their program offered electives in the management science department. However, this was most common in the tier 3 programs (42.86%), which was significantly more common than in tier 2 programs (14.29%) (p-value = .053). Likewise, 73% of programs offered electives in the Finance department, but tier 1 programs (88%) were significantly more likely to do so than both tier 2 (66.67%) and tier 3 (57.14%) programs (p-value = 0.100 and p-value = 0.037, respectively).

Prospective students should carefully consider the electives offered at each institution to ensure they align with their research interests. For example, a student interested in behavioral research may find it useful to attend an institution offering electives in the psychology department, while

students interested in archival research may be better served by taking electives in the economics or finance departments.

Beyond Course Requirements, What Other Deliverables Are
Required at Your Institution?
In satisfying the requirements for a terminal degree in accounting, universities require additional deliverables outside of course requirements. These
deliverables may take the form of additional paper requirements and/or
presentations. Of the universities represented in our survey, 56.67% of the
doctoral programs in accounting require a first year summer paper/presen-
tation, which is generally due at the end of the student's first year of residency. Likewise, 70% of the universities represented require a second year
summer paper/presentation. Almost half (43.33%) of the programs require
both a first and second year summer paper/presentation. Two students
indicated that their university requires a summer paper/presentation for
each year of residency.

In addition to summer papers/presentations, doctoral students in
accounting often must pass qualifying and/or comprehensive exams to
continue in the doctoral program. These exams generally are designed to
test the student's understanding of the seminars taken to date. Some students (8.33%) indicated that their university requires a first year qualifying/
comprehensive exam to be taken at the end of their first academic year.
More commonly, however, students are required to take a second year
qualifying/comprehensive exam (93.3%), typically occurring upon completion of their coursework. Interestingly, 100% of the participants representing tier 2 and tier 3 programs indicated that a written comprehensive exam
was required after a student's second year, while only 84% of the participants representing tier 1 programs indicated the same requirements
(p-value = 0.030 and p-value = 0.053, respectively). In fact, only one of the
tier 1 programs that did not require a second year written comprehensive
exam did so in the student's first year. This may suggest that some of the
programs in tier 1 do not find added value to having students take a
comprehensive exam. As discussed below, this may be because studying for
comprehensive exams can detract from a student's ability to produce
original research.[7]

Just as there are benefits and drawbacks to the number and types of
courses required in a doctoral program, there are benefits and drawbacks
to the number of deliverables required outside of coursework. For example,
one of the main benefits to a summer paper/presentation requirement is
that it gives students a chance to practice both their research skills and

presentation skills in front of faculty members and fellow doctoral students at their institution and receive feedback. This is a low-cost opportunity to improve a student's skills and practice learning how to take constructive criticism.

Summer papers can also turn into published research papers, which are helpful to students when they are on the job market. However, based on the survey data, there appears to be a negative correlation between the requirement to perform a second year paper and the number of published papers a student may have upon graduation. Further analysis shows that of the students indicating that a typical student has a published paper upon graduation, only 54% of those programs required a second year summer paper compared to 81% of the other programs. This may suggest that students have a better time publishing a paper upon graduation if they have the ability to focus on advancing their first year paper or another project, as opposed to starting an additional second year paper. A drawback to qualifying/comprehensive exams is that it may detract from a student's research productivity. Studying for a comprehensive exam can require students to study for months in order to be adequately prepared. While studying for these exams, students may find it difficult to progress their research streams.

Survey responses clearly indicate that there are significant differences between the courses and deliverables required at accounting doctoral institutions in the United States. The information above should provide students with a framework for understanding these differences and the frequencies with which various seminars are offered and deliverables are required. In addition to the information above, there are a number of other considerations which prospective students may want to factor in when making decisions about which doctoral program is best for them.

What Is the Expected Role of Qualifying/Comprehensive Exams?
As stated earlier, students often study for extended periods of time for qualifying/comprehensive exams at the expense of writing research papers. Institutions differ significantly on how they conduct examinations, and as noted above some tier 1 institutions have completely done away with these examinations. Some programs consider these exams to be a rite of passage that is required to show superior understanding of the course materials to date. Other institutions may find the benefits of these exams do not outweigh the costs. They are either moving them earlier in the students' coursework or simply doing away with the exam, which allows the students to spend more time on their dissertation and other research projects. Finally,

the content of these exams can differ significantly with some institutions focusing the exams on material derived from the accounting seminars while other institutions focus the exams on material from statistics or methodology courses.

How Often Are the Accounting Seminars and Electives Offered?
Some courses are very small and not offered on a routine basis. Institutions may only offer certain courses when there are enough students to warrant it. That being said, the coursework phase of a doctoral student's education can often extend into the third and fourth years simply because courses are offered infrequently. One potential benefit to courses being spread out is that students can focus and absorb a maximum amount of material per course. However, the obvious drawback is that when courses are spread out it can delay the dissertation phase of a doctoral student's education, which in turn delays the student's opportunities to graduate and seek employment.

Student Cohort Information

How Often Are Students Admitted to Your Institution?
When deciding which school to apply to, and when, it is important to keep in mind that not all accounting doctoral programs admit new students on a consistent schedule. For example, unlike some other academic programs, students generally are only admitted to an accounting doctoral program starting in the fall semester. Eighty-five percent of the students indicated that their programs admit new students once per year and 15% of the accounting doctoral programs admit students every other year. Tier 3 (35.71%) programs are more likely to admit students every other year than both tier 1 (4%) and tier 2 (14.29%) programs (p-value $= 0.008$ and p-value $= 0.076$, respectively).

How often an institution admits new doctoral students can be significant. There could be a variety of reasons why it is not in the best interest of many students to wait a whole year to begin a doctoral education. Also, if a doctoral program admits new students each year, then it is more likely that the institution will offer accounting courses on a more consistent basis. However, holding constant the number of students admitted per admission cycle, if a doctoral program admits new students every other year, then it is more likely that students will have a greater chance to develop relationships with faculty members because their time is not being split between that cohort and as many other cohorts. Nonetheless, the number of students in the cohort will also have a major influence on a student's ability to develop relationships with faculty, and as noted in the next section, doctoral programs that admit students every other year tend to have larger cohorts than doctoral programs that admit students every year.

How Many Students Are Admitted to Your Institution?
In addition to understanding when a program admits new students, it is also important to consider the number of students admitted in a given year (i.e., cohort size). Doctoral programs in accounting are very intimate. The median (mean) number of doctoral students admitted was 2.5 (2.73). The smallest average cohort size indicated was 1.5; the largest student cohort indicated was 5. The schools that admit students every year on average admit 2.6 new students per admission cycle. The programs that admit students every other year on average admit 3.7 new doctoral students per admission cycle. The timing of admission and the number of students admitted per cycle are highly correlated; therefore, programs that admit students every year admit fewer students than programs that admit students every other year.

In addition to the students in a single cohort, it may be worth noting the total size of a doctoral program in accounting. The median (mean) number of students in residence was 10 (10.6), with the smallest program size being one and the largest being 26. Tier 1 schools have on average 11.96 students in residence, which is significantly more than tier 2 programs' 9.24 students (p-value = .014). This is consistent with tier 1 programs graduating on average significantly more doctoral students in the past 10 years (24.92) than either tier 2 (17.80) or tier 3 (18.21) programs (p-value = 0.002 and p-value = 0.010, respectively) based on a review of the Hasselback Accounting Directory.

The schools that admit students every year have on average 11.1 doctoral students in residency at a given time while programs that admit students every other year have on average 7.9 doctoral students in residency. The timing of admission and the number of doctoral students in residency are highly correlated; therefore, programs that admit students every year, not surprisingly, have more students in residency than programs that admit students every other year. However, it is worth noting that this difference is not as large as one might expect because as noted above, programs that admit students every other year tend to admit more students per admission cycle. Table 2 offers descriptive statistics regarding the size of the programs represented in this survey.

For prospective doctoral students, it is important to keep in mind the size of their prospective cohort and the total number of students in residence while they attend a doctoral program. The major benefit to a smaller size program is that students should have a greater opportunity to work closely with faculty at that institution. However, the larger the size of the program, the more likely that the students will have the opportunity to connect with fellow doctoral students and make lasting working relationships that will likely span a much longer time period than a relationship with faculty members simply because of employment horizons. Another factor for the students to consider is that it may seem easier to gain admittance to programs with larger cohorts, simply because they admit more people. However, a larger cohort means more competition for faculty time, which may lead to lower matriculation rates. Therefore, it is important to consider a program's student-to-faculty ratio. On average, this ratio is .689, but it can range from a low of .11 to a high of 2.17. Tier 1 programs have a significantly higher student-to-faculty ratio (.7865) than tier 2 programs (.6065) (p-value = 0.059).

How Long Does It Typically Take Doctoral Students to Graduate at Your Institution?

Accounting doctoral programs involve a significant time investment. Prospective students often leave well-paying accounting careers to become a student. Typically, accounting doctoral students do not have the time and can be precluded from working outside the doctoral program. This may make it look attractive to find a doctoral program that generally graduates students in a shorter time period, and therefore would allow the student to quickly return to an income-earning phase of their life. However, the sacrifice of spending a few extra years in an accounting doctoral program allows the student to produce a well-developed research stream that will likely help them obtain a higher paying position at a research institution and in the long term, may prove to be better for their career. Therefore, a major consideration has to be how long it takes to graduate.

There was great variation to this question based on the survey results. The median (mean) number of years it takes doctoral students to graduate was 5 (4.89), with a minimum of three years and a maximum of 15 years. The results from this survey indicated that about 33% of students are expected to graduate in four years or less. This is consistent with Plumlee *et al.* (2006), which indicated an assumption of about 30% of students will graduate by their fourth year in a program. However, not surprisingly it takes students from tier 1 programs, which tend to focus more on developing a quality research stream, longer to graduate than students from tier 3 programs, on average (5.2 years vs. 4.29 years, respectively, p-value = 0.091). The students indicated that the median (mean) percent of students who graduate from their doctoral program in accounting was 90% (85.3%), ranging from a low of 5% and a high of 100%.

Recall that the data presented in this chapter are from current doctoral students. Current doctoral students may not have perfect information regarding long-term statistics such as the long-term percent of students that graduate and the average number of years it takes students to graduate. However, it appears that the students who participated in this survey have adequate knowledge regarding these statistics. We asked accounting doctoral program coordinators, who presumably have better long-term knowledge about a program, to indicate the percent of admitted students that graduate from their respective program and the number of years it takes an average student to graduate. When comparing the responses we obtained from the Ph.D. coordinators to the responses from students from the same respective programs, we do not note any significant differences. The Ph.D. coordinators indicated that the median (mean) percent of students that graduate from their program once admitted was 85% (84.2%), which is almost identical to the response of 90% (84.8%) from the students from the same programs.[8] The Ph.D. coordinators indicated that the median (mean) number of years it takes for doctoral students to graduate is 4.25 (4.4) years, which again is almost identical to the response of 4 (4.4) years from the students from the same programs.

Students should carefully consider the goals they have for a career in academia and the matriculation rates at specific institutions. A student should be honest with him/herself and determine whether they feel that they would be successful at a particular institution. If a student does not graduate from a doctoral institution and is unable to begin a career as a tenure track faculty member, it can be very disheartening to spend year(s) in a doctoral program just to seek employment the individual was already qualified to hold.

Student Research Support

How Often Do Students Attend Academic Conferences at Your Institution?
In addition to training received by faculty members at their institution, accounting doctoral students also receive valuable training at academic research conferences. Many doctoral students attend research conferences,

Table 2. Student Cohort Information.

				Median	Mean	Standard Deviation	Minimum	Maximum
Typical Cohort Size	1–2 Students	3 Students	4–5 Students	Median	Mean	Standard Deviation	Minimum	Maximum
	41.7%	38.3%	20.0%	2.50	2.73	0.85	1.50	5.00
Students in Residence	1–7 Students	8–14 Students	15–26 Students	Median	Mean	Standard Deviation	Minimum	Maximum
	15.0%	71.7%	13.3%	10.00	10.60	3.74	1.00	26.00
Years in Residence	<4 Years	4 Years	>4 Years	Median	Mean	Standard Deviation	Minimum	Maximum
	7.0%	26.3%	66.7%	5.00	4.89	1.59	3.00	15.00
Matriculation Rates	<50%	51–75%	76–100%	Median	Mean	Standard Deviation	Minimum	Maximum
	3.3%	16.7%	80.0%	90.0%	85.3%	18.1%	5.0%	100.0%

such as the American Accounting Association (AAA) annual meeting, and other AAA sectional or regional meetings. Schools differ on the number and type of conferences that they recommend to doctoral students. We asked student participants to indicate the number of conferences doctoral students typically attend throughout their residency. The median (mean) total number of conferences attended by doctoral students while in residency at their institution was 5 (5.54). The typical number of conferences attended ranged from 1.5 to 17.5. Tier 1 doctoral programs have each student attend 6.3 conferences on average, which is significantly more than the average of 4.29 (p-value = 0.052) attended by students from tier 3 doctoral programs.

Costs associated with attending these conferences can be well over $1,000 and are sometimes funded through the university, college/school (i.e., College of Business), or department; other times, students fund travel and other conference expenses themselves. We asked students to indicate the percent of conference travel funded by their institution. The median (mean) percentage of funding provided by the university (rather than by the student) for these conferences was 95% (87.3%). Travel costs covered by institutions ranged from 25% to 100%, with 45.9% of institutions funding all of the conference-related expenses. Interestingly, it does not appear that the percent of funded conference travel impacted the number of conferences a student typically attends. Not surprisingly, the percent of funding that a program provides for conference travel is negatively correlated with the program's number of students in residency and cohort size. Table 3 offers the frequency with which students indicated the number of conferences attended throughout residency and the percent of these travel costs covered by the institution.

Prospective students should ascertain from possible doctoral programs how often they are expected to attend a research conference and how this travel will be funded. A major benefit from attending multiple conferences is that students get to encounter research from accounting academics at other institutions, through both the doctoral consortium preceding the conference, and the conference itself. This should broaden the student's appreciation and understanding of accounting research. Additionally, students may have an opportunity to present their own research or discuss a research paper, which can lead to contacts for future employment. In fact, there appears to be a correlation between attending more research conferences and obtaining a job at a higher ranking research institution.[9] Another major benefit to attending multiple conferences is that students will get to meet faculty members and other doctoral students at institutions throughout the United States and world. For accounting academics who often work on research projects with multiple other academics, it is important to have the opportunities to create these working relationships.

While I am an Accounting Doctoral Student at Your Institution,
Who Can I Expect to Work With?
Students in a doctoral program typically work on research-related projects with one or more professors. The number and type of professors that students work with varies between schools as well as between individual students within those schools. However, doctoral students generally have one primary mentor, who often chairs their dissertation. The level of professor (assistant, associate, or full) that students work with depends on the institution and the individual. Students often have mentors in their area of research (or a similar area of research), so that students are able to learn from established researchers in their field of interest.

Assistant professors, who generally have graduated from a doctoral program within the past 10 years or less, have recent experience from their own doctoral program to bring to a mentoring relationship. Associate and full professors, who have generally been in academia for a longer period of time, can provide a different and perhaps more experienced perspective for students. These professors also generally have more time to devote to mentoring doctoral students, as they do not also have the pressure of trying to achieve tenure. One risk of having an untenured (assistant) professor as a mentor is that the professor may not be granted tenure, and may be forced to leave the institution before his/her mentee completes the doctoral program. Also, the assistant professor's focus on getting tenure could prevent them from devoting an appropriate amount of time to doctoral students. We asked participants to indicate how often each type of professor (assistant, associate, full, and other) is matched with a doctoral student as their primary mentor. On average, 18.9% of doctoral students are matched with an assistant professor as their primary mentor, 35% are matched with an associate professor as their primary mentor, and 57.3% are matched with a full professor as their primary mentor.[10]

In addition to their primary mentor, doctoral students often collaborate with other faculty members on research projects and co-authored papers. Collaborating with multiple faculty members at different levels can provide doctoral students with multiple perspectives and different styles of research. We asked participants to indicate how often a typical doctoral student collaborates with each type of professor (assistant, associate, full, and other). Results show that 43.5% of doctoral students collaborate with assistant professors, 45.5% collaborate with associate professors, and 55.4%

collaborate with full professors. The type of professor a student has as a primary mentor is highly correlated with the type of professor with which a student typically collaborates. This is indicative of students typically working with their mentor on research projects.

Will I Have Research Assistant Responsibilities at Your Institution?
Most students receive a stipend while enrolled in a doctoral program. In exchange for this stipend, students are expected to work as either a research assistant, perform teaching duties, or both. As a research assistant, students are assigned to one or more faculty members to assist them with research projects. In some instances, these research assistantships result in co-authored papers; other research assistantships do not.

We asked participants to indicate how many years a typical doctoral student is assigned as a "research assistant" while in residence at their institutions. Approximately 88.8% of our respondents indicated that their program required students to serve as a research assistant during their doctoral education, which is slightly higher than Imhoff's (1988), which indicated 78.34% of programs. Responses indicate that doctoral students spend a median (mean) of 3 (2.8) years assigned as a research assistant while enrolled in the doctoral program. The total number of years ranges from a low of zero to a high of five years. Tier 3 programs on average assigned their students as research assistants for 1.81 years, which is significantly shorter than both tier 1 (3.02 years) and tier 2 (3.29 years) programs (p-value = 0.04043 and p-value = 0.016, respectively).

A total of 44.4% of the participants responding indicated that the typical student is assigned as a research assistant for four or five years while in residency at their institution. Dividing the number of years a student is assigned as a research assistant by the average number of years in residency shows that on average, students act as a research assistant for 57.3% of their residency. It is worth noting that our survey results indicate that the number of years a student serves as a research assistant is negatively correlated with the number of students admitted in a single cohort. This makes sense because holding constant the research assistant needs of a doctoral program, programs with larger cohorts are spreading this need out among more students.

Students who have the opportunity to be a research assistant often have the benefits of creating close working relationships with faculty members at their institution. If the student is a research assistant for the same professor for multiple consecutive semesters, this relationship is often strengthened. Imhoff (1988) states that working as a research assistant for a faculty

Table 3. Research Support Information.

Conferences Attended	<4	4–7	>7	Median	Mean	Standard Deviation	Minimum	Maximum
	25.0%	53.6%	21.4%	5.00	5.54	2.87	1.50	17.50
Funded Conference Travel	<50%	51–75%	76–100%	Median	Mean	Standard Deviation	Minimum	Maximum
	7.3%	10.9%	81.8%	95.0%	87.3%	17.7%	25.0%	100.0%
Mentoring Faculty	<50%	51–75%	76–100%	Median	Mean	Standard Deviation	Minimum	Maximum
Assistant	87.7%	3.5%	8.8%	0.0%	18.9%	29.7%	0.0%	100.0%
Associate	82.5%	5.3%	12.3%	33.0%	35.0%	28.3%	0.0%	100.0%
Full	45.6%	17.5%	36.8%	60.0%	57.3%	33.1%	0.0%	100.0%
Faculty Collaborations	<50%	51–75%	76–100%	Median	Mean	Standard Deviation	Minimum	Maximum
Assistant	70.2%	10.5%	19.3%	34.0%	43.5%	30.0%	0.0%	100.0%
Associate	68.4%	10.5%	21.1%	40.0%	45.5%	27.9%	0.0%	100.0%
Full	49.1%	15.8%	35.1%	60.0%	54.4%	33.4%	0.0%	100.0%
Research Assignment in Years	0 Years	1–3 Years	>3 Years	Median	Mean	Standard Deviation	Minimum	Maximum
	11.1%	44.4%	44.4%	3.00	2.81	1.62	0.00	5.00
Research Papers	0	1–2	>2	Median	Mean	Standard Deviation	Minimum	Maximum
Published	58.6%	41.4%	0.0%	0.00	0.32	0.42	0.00	1.50
Under Review	6.9%	93.1%	0.0%	1.00	1.19	0.51	0.00	2.00
Working Papers	0.0%	50.0%	50.0%	2.25	2.45	0.90	1.00	4.50

member with an established research record could be one of the most beneficial learning experiences in the student's Ph.D. program. Students should
take advantage of opportunities to work with faculty. As stated earlier,
faculty members often take the opportunity of having a research assistant
to develop a co-authored paper with the student. This can be very beneficial in the student's career. However, other faculty members, especially if
the research assistant responsibilities are short term, will request that the
student perform specific duties for the professor's existing projects that are
less likely to lead to co-authored opportunities, such as data collection.
Students should inquire whether they will likely serve as a research assistant
to one faculty member and have the opportunity to develop a long-term
working relationship with that faculty member or if they will likely work
for multiple faculty members for shorter durations.

What Is the Typical Student's Research Portfolio Look
Like upon Graduation at Your Institution?
Published papers are important for achieving tenure at an academic institution. These papers often take years to complete, so the earlier a student
starts the process, the better the likelihood they will have enough published
research to obtain tenure. Therefore, the more quality research projects a
student develops during their doctoral program the better. Doctoral students often have several projects at various stages (published papers, working papers under review, and/or working papers with data) at the time of
graduation. Published papers represent work that has been accepted at a
journal; working papers under review have been submitted to a journal, but
have not yet been accepted; and working papers with data represent manuscripts that include data and are not currently under review at a journal.

   Based on responses received from study participants, students have a
median (mean) of 0 (0.3) published papers, 1 (1.19) working paper under
review, and 2.25 (2.45) working papers with data when they complete their
terminal degree. The maximum number of published papers for a typical
doctoral student indicated by participants in our survey was 1.5.[11] For
working papers under review, responses ranged from a low of zero to a
high of two. Tier 1 programs have students that graduate with an average
of 1.31 working papers under review, which is significantly more than tier 3
programs' students, which graduate with an average of 1 working paper
under review (p-value = 0.078). Tier 1 institutions appear to expect students
to have a portfolio of research projects that have been developed thoroughly enough to be submitted to a journal for review, which may account
for students taking longer to graduate from a tier 1 program. For working

papers with data, responses ranged from a low of 1 to a high of 4.5. The average number of total papers at all three stages ranged from a low of 1 to a high of 7. Table 3 displays this information.

As suggested before, it is possible that current students are not the best source of information for long-term statistics such as in this case regarding an average student's research portfolio at the time of graduation. However, as before it appears that when we look at the subsample of doctoral programs in which we received responses from both doctoral program coordinators and current doctoral students, student responses mirror those of doctoral program coordinators, who should have a better long-term picture for their program. Specifically, program coordinators indicated that their students have a median (mean) of 0.5 (0.6) published papers, 1 (1.1) working paper under review, and 2 (2.1) working papers with data when they complete their terminal degree. That is similar to the responses obtained from students from the same respective programs who indicated that students have a median (mean) of 0.5 (0.4) published papers, 1.5 (1.4) working papers under review, and 2.5 (2.6) working papers with data when they complete their terminal degree.

Student Teaching

How Much Teaching Experience Do Students Obtain at Your Institution?
Two of the major components of an accounting academics' career are teaching and research. Typically, a doctoral degree in accounting is designed to educate students to become researchers; however, most doctoral programs offer their students a chance to gain experience teaching. Prospective students should carefully consider their own personal goals when deciding which doctoral program to attend. The greater the teaching load, the less time available to work on and improve a student's research; however, if a student wants to gain teaching experience, they should attend an institution that affords such an opportunity. Another consideration should be the level of courses expected to be taught. In general, the higher the course level, the greater the time expected to prepare to teach the course. For example, a senior level accounting course is generally expected to take more time to prepare to teach than a freshman level course.

Doctoral programs require different amounts, and types, of teaching. In some programs, doctoral students teach their own courses, while in other programs, doctoral students act as teaching assistants (TAs). The amount of teaching and type of courses taught varies between programs as well.

Some programs require teaching every semester, while others require teaching as little as one semester. Some programs have doctoral students teaching courses at the undergraduate level, while others have students teaching at the graduate level.

Another variation on teaching between doctoral programs is the number of different courses ("preps") a doctoral student teaches. Some schools require students to teach one course throughout their time in the doctoral program (e.g., introductory financial accounting) although they may teach this course multiple times. Other schools require students to teach multiple different courses (e.g., introductory financial accounting, introductory managerial accounting). The median (mean) number of different course preps a doctoral student teaches during his/her program is 1 (2.22). Our results suggest that approximately 91.4% of the doctoral programs require some form of teaching during the student's doctoral education. This is slightly higher than Behn et al. (2008) and Imhoff's (1988), which suggested 80% and 83.8% of programs require students to teach, respectively. The median (mean) number of sections a doctoral student teaches during their program is 2 (3.42). However, there is a large standard deviation for each of these questions (3.95 for number of different course preps and 3.35 for number of sections). Further analysis shows that students at tier 1 programs teach significantly fewer sections (2.19) than both tier 2 (3.93) and tier 3 (4.88) programs (p-value = 0.079 and p-value = 0.019, respectively). The median (mean) percent of courses taught to freshman or sophomore level classes is 70% (61.5%). The median (mean) percent of courses taught to junior or senior level classes is 30% (38.5%). The median (mean) percent of courses taught to graduate level classes is 0% (2.4%). Tier 2 programs appear to be significantly less likely to require upper level classes be taught by their doctoral students (26.71%) than tier 1 (45.5%) and tier 3 (46.92%) programs (p-value = 0.062 and p-value = 0.076, respectively). Table 4 provides descriptive information relating to the teaching expectations of doctoral students.

Job Placements

Where Do Graduates from Your Institution Typically Obtain Tenure Track Faculty Positions?
After graduating with a terminal degree in accounting, students generally find employment in tenure track positions at various colleges and universities. Where a student will ultimately be employed as a faculty member is one important consideration in selecting a doctoral program. To determine

the types of schools where students obtain employment, we gathered data from Hasselback Accounting Faculty Directory[12] listing the students who graduated from each doctoral degree granting institution in the past 10 years and where they are currently employed.[13] We then used the BYU rankings[14] to rank institutions.

Based on a review of the Hasselback Accounting Directory, from 2003 to 2013, Panel A of Table 5 shows that 19.3% of doctoral graduates are placed at a top 50 academic research institution. Students graduating from tier 1 doctoral programs are placed at a top 50 academic program 30.7% of the time while tier 2 and tier 3 graduates are placed at these programs 11.2% and 3.5% of the time, respectively. Almost 60% of graduates from a tier 1 doctoral program are placed at a top 150 academic research institution compared to just under 40% and 10.2% for tier 2 and tier 3 doctoral programs. These numbers clearly support that, on average, to be placed at a higher ranked research institution a student is better served attending a tier 1 doctoral program. In fact, Table 5 Panel B shows that of the current faculty members at a top 50 academic research institution, 78.9% obtained their doctoral degree from a tier 1 doctoral program even though tier 1 doctoral program graduates represent 49.8% of all doctoral graduates.

Not surprisingly, there is a high correlation between the doctoral program tier and being placed at a better ranking research institution. We also observe additional correlations between our doctoral program characteristics and placement at better ranking institutions. However, many of these correlations can also be seen in our discussion of the differences between tiers above. For example, it appears that teaching more (preps and sections), which is more likely to be encountered in a tier 3 program, leads to placements at lower ranking research institutions. On the other hand, serving more years as a research assistant or having more papers under review at the time of graduation is correlated with placement at better ranking institutions. This finding again is not surprising because tier 1 institutions tend to assign students as a research assistant for a greater number of years and tier 1 students have more papers under review at graduation.

Clearly, if a student's goal is to place at a high ranking research institution, he or she would be better served attending a tier 1 doctoral program. However, there are some tier 1 programs that do not place their students at high ranking research institutions and there are tier 2 and tier 3 programs that do place their students at high ranking institutions. Therefore, it would be insightful to understand within each tier, if there are doctoral program characteristics that likely lead to better placement. That is, controlling for what tier a doctoral program is in, what other factors might influence a student's placement. To better understand this relationship, ideally, we would perform a statistical regression controlling for such factors as program tier and student-to-faculty ratio. To run a statistical regression, we would need appropriate sample sizes for any conclusions to be valid. However, because there are less than 100 doctoral programs in the United States graduating on average two accounting doctoral students per year, the sample size for this analysis could lead to drawing faulty conclusions.

Although it is not possible to statistically draw conclusions, there are a couple of insights worth noting. First, although it is hard to say what courses will lead to better placement at a research university, student relationships with the faculty at their institution will play a tremendous role in future placement opportunities. Therefore, as students progress through coursework and perform various research assistant functions for faculty members, fostering these relationships in a positive manner can improve future placements. Second, fostering the relationship with the student's fellow cohort and other students at the institution can also positively affect placement opportunities. Upon obtaining a faculty position, new faculty members are asked often "is there anybody at your Alma mater we should consider for this position?" Third, attending conferences is the best way to foster relationships with faculty members at other institutions and because students will not likely obtain a faculty position at their doctoral degree granting institutions, these relationships will go a long way in obtaining a faculty position. Finally, remember that students are judged on research productivity when obtaining their first position. Therefore, staying an additional year in a doctoral program to advance a few research projects may be a short-term sacrifice, but it will likely have long-term rewards.

CONCLUSION

There are many commonalities and differences between doctoral programs in accounting. Prospective doctoral students and even doctoral program coordinators could benefit from understanding how these various doctoral programs are designed. Students should consider many things such as a school's placement record after graduation, the program's reputation in academia, the location of the university, and other factors. The purpose of this chapter is to provide a source of information detailing structural differences (e.g., types of seminars, support for travel, cohort information) among doctoral programs in accounting.

Table 4. Student Teaching Information.

Courses (Preps)	0	1–2	>2	Median	Mean	Standard Deviation	Minimum	Maximum
	8.6%	82.8%	8.6%	1.00	2.22	3.95	0.00	24.00
Sections	0	1–2	>2	Median	Mean	Standard Deviation	Minimum	Maximum
	8.6%	55.2%	36.2%	2.00	3.42	3.35	0.00	12.00
Courses Taught	<50%	51–75%	76–100%	Median	Mean	Standard Deviation	Minimum	Maximum
Freshmen/Sophomores	43.6%	12.7%	43.6%	70.0%	59.3%	35.6%	0.0%	100.0%
Juniors/Seniors	80.0%	1.8%	18.2%	30.0%	37.8%	32.2%	0.0%	100.0%
Graduate Courses	100.0%	0.0%	0.0%	0.0%	1.9%	6.3%	0.0%	30.0%

Table 5. Student Placement Information.

Panel A – Of the students graduating with a doctoral degree from each tier, the percent who placed at each university ranking.

	Accounting Research Ranking: Ranking for All Publications 2014 (BYU)									
	1–50	51–100	101–150	151–200	201–250	251–300	301–350	351–400	Over 400	Total
Overall	19.3%	11.7%	12.5%	6.5%	5.0%	4.2%	4.7%	6.5%	29.4%	100%
Tier 1	30.7%	16.4%	12.8%	4.2%	3.9%	3.2%	4.0%	4.3%	20.5%	100%
Tier 2	11.2%	10.2%	17.9%	9.4%	6.7%	5.1%	5.6%	7.8%	26.2%	100%
Tier 3	3.5%	2.7%	3.9%	8.2%	5.1%	5.5%	5.1%	10.2%	55.7%	100%

For example, out of the 623 students graduating in the past 10 years from a tier 1 program, 191 (30.7%) of them are currently placed at a top 50 research university.

Panel B – Of the students placed at each university ranking, the percent who obtained a doctoral degree from each doctoral program tier

	Accounting Research Ranking: Ranking for all Publications 2014 (BYU)									
	Overall	1–50	51–100	101–150	151–200	201–250	251–300	301–350	351–400	Over 400
Tier 1	49.8%	78.9%	69.4%	51.0%	31.7%	38.7%	37.7%	42.4%	32.9%	34.8%
Tier 2	29.9%	17.4%	25.9%	42.7%	42.7%	40.3%	35.8%	35.6%	35.4%	26.6%
Tier 3	20.4%	3.7%	4.8%	6.4%	25.6%	21.0%	26.4%	22.0%	31.7%	38.6%
Total	100%	100%	100%	100%	100%	100%	100%	100%	100%	100%

For example, out of the 242 students graduating in the past 10 years currently placed at a top 50 research university, 191 (78.9%) of them graduated from a tier 1 program.

Although most, if not all, doctoral programs in accounting consist of a coursework stage and a dissertation stage, the results of this survey show that there are many differences between the courses required. These differences include things such as the number of accounting seminars required within the program and how these various seminars are designed. Some programs separate their seminars based on methodologies (e.g., archival research, behavior research), while others separate their seminars based on subject matter (e.g., audit, tax). In addition to the differences in courses offered within the accounting departments, doctoral programs also differ on which other departments their students take elective courses (e.g., finance, psychology, math).

Other notable differences between doctoral programs in accounting, which may be of importance to prospective doctoral students, are the level of research support offered at various programs and with whom the doctoral students are collaborating on research projects. Some programs provide students complete financial support for travel to research conferences, while other programs place some, if not all, of the financial burden on the students. Some universities' doctoral students work and collaborate with experienced tenured professors, while others work with recent doctoral graduates who are currently untenured faculty. Finally, it is important to note that doctoral programs vary greatly on the teaching load expected of their doctoral students while in the program.

As with all studies, there are some important caveats to consider with this manuscript. First, we administered the survey used for the present study to current doctoral students in accounting at 60 different doctoral programs. Although it is reasonable that they are exceptionally well aware of the current program requirements at their institutions, these requirements may change. Second, it is important to understand that all doctoral student experiences are different, even for students attending the same institution. We instructed the participants for this study to respond as a "typical student" in their respective program, so the intent is that the data reflect the perceived average student experience. However, having one student from each doctoral program respond to our survey is a limitation of our study, as having different student participants could have yielded different insights into their respective programs.

For prospective students deciding to pursue a doctoral education in accounting, one of the most important decisions they will make is which program to attend. The information provided in this chapter should help potential doctoral students by identifying a number of variables that should be researched when choosing an institution to attend, as well as current norms for these variables. For the prospective doctoral students reading this chapter, we wish you luck on this intellectually exciting and rewarding endeavor.

NOTES

1. For additional information about the ADS program, visit the ADS website (http://www.adsphd.org).

2. Students who were in their fourth year of the doctoral program were our target participants. We believe that this allows for enough time in the program to have an understanding of typical student experiences, but also targets students who are not far removed from coursework and the comprehensive exam process. As there are generally a small number of students in each year of the program, we chose to request participation from one student per school. If we did not receive a response from the first participant we contacted, we contacted an alternate participant.

3. In addition to having current students respond to the survey about doctoral program characteristics, we also invited doctoral program coordinators to participate for comparison purposes. Thirty-three program coordinators responded to the survey, with 23 being from institutions in which we received student responses as well. We use the student responses for the primary analysis in this chapter because the goal of the chapter is to provide a student perspective on their respective doctoral programs. However, we used the doctoral program coordinators' responses to help validate some of the data collected from students.

4. There are differences within each tier regarding doctoral program characteristics, meaning, not all tier 1 programs are the same. This additional analysis is meant to describe differences between tiers, where, on average a tier 1 program is designed differently than an average tier 2 or tier 3 program. This additional analysis is restricted to program characteristics that significantly differ between tiers, meaning that there is less than a 10% chance that we conclude there is a difference between tiers when in fact there is not.

5. Appendix B presents a correlation table of select variables collected in the survey.

6. Not surprisingly this variable is highly correlated with the type of seminars offered at each institution. The more likely a student was to indicate that their seminars were subject-based by indicating a higher number on this question, the more likely they were to indicate having subject-based seminars in tax, audit, financial accounting, and managerial accounting. Conversely, a higher number on this scale was negatively correlated with the program offering research methodology-based seminars in archival, behavioral, and analytical research methodologies (see Appendix B).

7. Some students indicated additional requirements for graduation that are designed to enhance the expertise of the students. For example, one student indicated that their university requires SAS certification. SAS is a statistical software package used for data analysis.

8. Recall that we received responses from students representing 60 different doctoral programs. Doctoral program coordinator responses represent 33 different doctoral programs. However, we received both student responses and doctoral program coordinator responses that represent 23 different programs. For comparison between doctoral student responses and doctoral program coordinator responses, we used the latter subset.

9. Discussed in more detail later, we obtained placement data for the past 10 years from each of the institutions represented in our survey from Hasselback (2012). Using these data and the BYU rankings of each institution, we calculated an "average placement" score for each program. A lower score represents on average that a program places their students at higher ranking research institutions.

10. Percentages do not add up to exactly 100% due to some participants responding a total of more than 100%. This could be due to some students having co-mentors (i.e., more than one primary mentor). However, the majority of participants responded with amounts that totaled 100% across the categories (assistant professor, associate professor, full professor, and other).

11. Note that this number represents an average of publications for students graduating from this institution.

12. This information was obtained at http://www.jrhasselback.com/AtgDoct/XSchDoct.pdf. The most recent version of this listing was May 29, 2014, at the time of this chapter's preparation.

13. We also analyzed data based on graduations within the past five years, and using all the years available listed in the Hasselback Accounting Faculty Directory. We present 10-year data in this section, because five-year data does not allow for a sufficient sample size on which to base conclusions, and using all years available listed results in samples for some schools being much greater than others. There were minimal differences when comparing the data presented to all graduations listed.

14. This information was obtained at http://www.byuaccounting.net/rankings/univrank/rank_university.php?qurank=All&sortorder=ranking6. The most recent version of this listing was 2014 at the time of this chapter's preparation.

ACKNOWLEDGMENT

The authors would like to thank Erin Hamilton and John Reisch for their helpful comments and suggestions on an earlier version of this manuscript. In addition we would like to thank the two anonymous reviewers for their valuable comments and the co-editor, Tim Rupert.

REFERENCES

Behn, B. K., Carnes, G. A., Krull, G. W. Jr., Stocks, K. D., & Reckers, P. M. J. (2008). Accounting doctoral education − 2007 A report of the joint AAA/APLG/FSA doctoral education committee. *Issues in Accounting Education, 23*, 357−367.

Bergner, J. (2009). Pursuing a Ph.D. in Accounting: Walking in with your eyes open. *Journal of Accountancy Web-exclusive.* Retrieved from http://www.journalofaccountancy.com/news/2009/mar/pursuingaphdinaccounting.html

Beyer, B., Herrmann, D., Meek, G. K., & Rapley, E. T. (2010). What it means to be an accounting professor: A concise career guide for doctoral students in accounting. *Issues in Accounting Education, 25*, 227−244.

Cho, C. H., Roberts, R. W., & Roberts, S. K. (2008). Chinese students in US accounting and business PhD programs: Educational, political and social considerations. *Critical Perspectives in Accounting, 19*, 199−216.

Hasselback, J. R. (2012). *Accounting faculty directory* (35th ed.). Upper Saddle River, NJ: Pearson Prentice Hall.

Hermanson, D. R. (2008). What I have learned so far: Observations on managing an academic accounting career. *Issues in Accounting Education, 23*, 53−66.

Imhoff, E. A. (1988). Planning academic accounting careers. *Issues in Accounting Education, 3*, 286−301.

McGee, R. W. (1999). What's wrong with the curriculum in accounting PhD programs? Five case studies viewed from the perspectives of economics and ethics. *Journal of Accounting, Ethics & Public Policy, 2*, 1−12.

Plumlee, R. D., Kachelmeier, S. J., Madeo, S. A., Pratt, J. J., & Krull., G. (2006). Assessing the shortage of accounting faculty. *Issues in Accounting Education, 21*, 113−125.

Urbancic, F. (2008). A multiattributes approach for ranking PhD programs. *Journal of Education for Business, 83*, 339−346.

APPENDIX A

Survey Instrument

Variable Names
COURSE REQUIREMENTS

1. How many **seminars** do the Accounting Ph.D. students take at your
institution which are **offered through the accounting department**?
AccSem

2. Are the **accounting seminars** at your institution methodology-based (e.g.,
archival, experimental economics, behavioral) or subject-based (e.g., audit,
financial accounting)? (*AccStructure*)

Methodology-Based										Subject-Based
1	2	3	4	5	6	7	8	9	10	11

3. Indicate below the accounting seminars offered at your institution through the accounting
department. Please select all that apply. The number of seminars selected should equal the
number of seminars you indicated above as being offered at your institution through the
accounting department.

☐ Introduction to Accounting Research (Methodology-Based) (*IntroMethod*)
☐ Introduction to Accounting Research (Subject-Based) (*IntroSubject*)
☐ Taxation Research (Subject-Based) (*Tax*)
☐ Audit Research (Subject-Based) (*Audit*)
☐ Financial Accounting Research (Subject-Based) (*Financial*)
☐ Managerial Accounting Research (Subject-Based) (*Managerial*)
☐ Archival Research (Methodology-Based) (*Archival*)
☐ Behavioral Research (Methodology-Based) (*Behavioral*)
☐ Experimental Economics Research (Methodology-Based) (*ExperimentalEcon*)
☐ Analytical Research (Methodology-Based) (*Analytical*)
☐ Other

4. Please indicate the department which students typically take core courses and elective
courses other than accounting seminars when fulfilling the requirements for a Ph.D. in
Accounting at your institution. Please select all that apply.

☐ Economics Department (*Economics*)
☐ Management Science Department (*MgtScience*)
☐ Marketing Department (*Marketing*)
☐ Psychology Department (*Psychology*)
☐ Finance Department (*Finance*)
☐ Other

NON-COURSE DELIVERABLES

1. In addition to the course requirements, please indicate below the deliverables required at your institution in order to fulfill the requirements for a Ph.D. in Accounting.

☐ First Year Summer Paper (*FirstSummer*)
☐ Second Year Summer Paper (*SecondSummer*)
☐ First Year Qualifying/Comprehensive Exam (Oral) (*FirstYearExamOral*)
☐ First Year Qualifying/Comprehensive Exam (Written) (*FirstYearExamWritten*)
☐ Second Year Qualifying/Comprehensive Exam (Oral) (*SecondYearExamOral*)
☐ Second Year Qualifying/Comprehensive Exam (Written) (*SecondYearExamWritten*)
☐ Dissertation Proposal Defense (*DissProposal*)
☐ Dissertation Final Defense (*DissDefense*)
☐ Other

STUDENT COHORT INFORMATION

1. Please indicate below how often your institution typically admits new Ph.D. students into the Ph.D. program. *AdmissionCycle*

○ Every Semester (fall and spring)
○ Every Year
○ Every Other Year
○ Other

2. Please indicate below the typical size of each cohort.

CohortSize   _____

3. Please indicate below the number of accounting Ph.D. students **currently in residence** at your institution (in total).

ResidenceSize   _____

4. Please indicate below the number of accounting Ph.D. students **not currently in residence** at your institution (i.e., took employment ABD) (in total).

ABDSize   _____

5. Please indicate below the typical number of years accounting Ph.D. students are in residence at your institution.

YearstoGraduate   _____

6. Please indicate below the matriculation rate of the accounting Ph.D. students at your institution, that is, the percent of students who begin the Ph.D. program and eventually graduate from your institution with a Ph.D. in Accounting (0–100%).

MatriculationRate   ____%

STUDENT RESEARCH SUPPORT

1. Please indicate below how many conferences the accounting Ph.D. students typically attend **throughout their residency** at your institution (not per year).

ConferencesAttended _____

2. Please indicate below the percent of the above conference travel which is funded by your institution (as opposed to covered by the students out of pocket) (0–100%).

ConFunding ____%

3. Please indicate below how often each type of professor is matched with an accounting Ph.D. student as their **primary mentor**.

Assistant Professor (*AssistantProf*) ____%

Associate Professor (*AssociateProf*) ____%

Full Professor (*FullProf*) ____%

Other _____ ____%

4. Please indicate below how often a typical accounting Ph.D. student collaborates with each type of professor.

Assistant Professor (*ColAssistant*) ____%

Associate Professor (*ColAssociate*) ____%

Full Professor (*ColFull*) ____%

Other _____ ____%

5. Please indicate below how many years a typical accounting Ph.D. student is assigned as a "Research Assistant" while in residence at your institution.

RAYears _____

6. Please indicate below the number of research projects a typical accounting Ph.D. student has at the time of graduation from your institution.

Published Papers (*PupPapers*) _____

Papers Under-Review (*UnderReview*) _____

Working Papers with Data (*WorkingPapers*) _____

STUDENT TEACHING EXPERIENCE

1. Please indicate below how many DIFFERENT COURSES a typical Ph.D. student at your institution is required to teach while enrolled in residency.

Preperations   _____

2. Please indicate below how many SECTIONS a typical Ph.D. student at your institution is required to teach while enrolled in residency.

Sections   _____

3. Please indicate below how often a typical accounting Ph.D. student is asked to teach the following level courses in accounting.

Freshman and Sophomore Level Courses (*Lowerlevel*)   ____%

Junior and Senior Level Courses (*Upperlevel*)   ____%

Graduate Level Courses (*Graduate*)   ____%

APPENDIX B

Table B1. Correlation Table.[a]

Category	Variable Name	Correlated Variables
Non-survey variables	*BYURank*	BYUTercile**, AvgPlacement**, (NumofGrads)** AdmissionCycle*, (ConferencesAttended)*, (RAY Years)*, (UnderReview)*, Sections*
	BYUTercile	BYURank**, AvgPlacement**, (NumofGrads)** (Analytical)*, (Finance), Second YearExamWritten* AdmissionCycle**, (ConferencesAttended)*, Sections*
	AvgPlacement	BYURank**, BYUTercile**, (Analytical)** MgtScience*, DissProposal*, AdmissionCycle* CohortSize**, (ConferencesAttended)*, Sections**
	NumofGrads	(BYURank)**, (BYUTercile)**, Behavioral* Finance*, ResidenceSize**, UnderReview*
	Faculty	(StudentFacultyRatio)**, YearstoGraduate**
	StudentFacultyRatio	(Faculty)**, Economics*, Finance* (AdmissionCycle)*, CohortSize** ResidenceSize**, (ConFunding)**, (ColAssistant)*
Course requirements	*AccSem*	(Behavioral)*, MatriculationRate*, FullProf*
	AccStructure	(IntroMethod)*, Tax**, Audit** Financial**, Managerial**, (Archival)** (Behavioral)**, (Analytical)*, Economics** (Lowerlevel)*
	IntroMethod	(AccStructure)*, (Economics)*
	IntroSubject	FirstSummer**
	Tax	AccStructure**, Financial*, (Lowerlevel)*
	Audit	AccStructure**, (Analytical)*
	Financial	AccStructure**, Tax*, Managerial** (Archival)**, (Behavioral)*, Economics** UnderReview*
	Managerial	AccStructure**, Financial**, (Archival)* (Behavioral)*, Economics*, FirstYearExamWritten* SecondYearExamOral**
	Archival	(AccStructure)**, (Financial)**, (Managerial)* (Economics)*, (FirstSummer)*
	Behavioral	Numo fGrads*, (AccSem)*, (AccStructure)** (Financial)*, (Managerial)*, Psychology*

(Continued)

Category	Variable Name	Correlated Variables
		(SecondSummer)**, (FirstYearExamWritten)* CohorSize*, (YearstoGraduate)*
	ExperimentalEcon	ColAssistant*, ColAssociate*
	Analytical	(BYUTercile)*, (AvgPlacement)**, (AccStructure)*
		(Audit)*, Finance*, YearstoGraduate* AssistantProf**
	Economics	StudentFacultyRatio*. AccStructure**, (IntroMethod)*
		Financial**, Managerial**, (Archival)* Finance*, FirstSummer**, SecondSummer* ResidenceSize*, (FullProf)*
	MgtScience	AvgPlacement*, AdmissionCycle*, PupPapers*
	Marketing	(Finance)**, FirstYearExamWritten*, AdmissionCycle*
		(ColAssociate)*, Graduate**
	Psychology	Behavioral*
	Finance	(BYUTercile)*, NumofGrads*, StudentFacultyRatio*
		Analytical*, Economics*, (Marketing)** (AdmissionCycle)**, (Preparations)*, (Graduate)**
Non-course	*FirstSummer*	IntroSubject**, (Archival)*, Economics**
deliverables	*SecondSummer*	(Behavioral)**, Economics*, ResidenceSize* (PupPapers)*, (Graduate)**
	FirstYearExamOral	
	FirstYearExamWritten	Managerial**, (Behavioral)*, Marketing*
	SecondYearExamOral	Managerial**, ABDSize*, Preparations*
	SecondYearExamWritten	BYUTercile*, DissProposal*
	DissProposal	AvgPlacement*, SecondYearExamWritten*
	DissDefense	
Student cohort	*AdmissionCycle*	BYURank**, BYUTercile**, AvgPlacement*
information		(StudentFacultyRatio)*, MgtScience*, Marketing*
		(Finance)**, CohortSize**, (ResidenceSize)* Graduate**
	CohortSize	AvgPlacement**, StudentFacultyRatio**, Behavioral*
		AdmissionCycle**, ResidenceSize**, (ConFunding)**
		(RAYears)*
	ResidenceSize	NumofGrads**, StudentFacultyRatio**, Economics*

(*Continued*)

Category	Variable Name	Correlated Variables
		SecondSummer*, (AdmissionCycle)*, CohortSize**
		(ConFunding)**, (ColAssistant)*, (ColFull)*
	ABDSize	SecondYearExamOral*
	YearstoGraduate	Faculty**, (Behavioral)*, Analytical*
		(ColFull)*, (WorkingPapers)*
	MatriculationRate	AccSem*
Student research support	*ConferencesAttended*	(BYURank)*, (BYUTercile)*, (AvgPlacement)*
		(AssistantProf)*
	ConFunding	(StudentFacultyRatio)**, (CohortSize)**, (ResidenceSize)**
		ColAssistant*
	AssistantProf	Analytical**, (ConferencesAttended)*, ColAssistant**
	AssociateProf	ColAssociate**
	FullProf	AccSem*, (Economics)*, ColFull**
		Lowerlevel**, Graduate*
	ColAssistant	(StudentFacultyRatio)*, ExperimentalEcon*, (ResidenceSize)*
		ConFunding*, AssistantProf**, ColAssociate**
		ColFull*
	ColAssociate	ExperimentalEcon*, (Marketing)*, AssociateProf**
		ColAssistant**, ColFull**
	ColFull	(Residence Size)*, (YeartoGraduate)*, FullProf**
		ColAssistant*, ColAssociate**
	RAYears	(BYURank)*, (CohortSize)**
	PupPapers	MgtScience*, (SecondSummer)*
	UnderReview	(BYURank)*, NumofGrads*, Financial*
		(Lowerlevel)*
	WorkingPapers	(YearstoGraduate)*, (Graduate)*
Student teaching experience	*Preparations*	(Finance)*, SecondYearExamOral*, Sections**
	Sections	BYURank*, BYUTercile*, AvgPlacement**
		Preparations**
	Lowerlevel	(AccStructure)*, (Tax)*, FullProf**
		(UnderReview)*, (Upperlevel)*
	Upperlevel	(Lowerlevel)*
	Graduate	Marketing**, (Finance)**, (SecondSummer)**
		AdmissionCycle**, FullProf*, (WorkingPapers)*

[a]Survey variables are defined in Appendix A "Survey Instrument."
**Positive (negative) correlation is significant at the 0.01 level (two-tailed).
*Positive (negative) correlation is significant at the 0.05 level (two-tailed).

PEDAGOGICAL TRAINING IN PH.D. PROGRAMS: HOW DOES ACCOUNTING COMPARE TO SIMILAR DISCIPLINES?

Ira Abdullah, Alisa G. Brink, C. Kevin Eller and Andrea Gouldman

ABSTRACT

Purpose — *We examine and compare current practices in teaching preparation in U.S. accounting, finance, management, and economics doctoral programs.*

Methodology/approach — *We conduct an anonymous online survey of the pedagogical training practices experienced by Ph.D. students in accounting, finance, management, and economics programs in the United States.*

Findings — *Results indicate that accounting, finance, and management perform similarly with respect to providing doctoral students with first-hand teaching experience and requiring for-credit courses in teacher training. Accounting and management appear to utilize doctoral students as teaching assistants less than the other disciplines. A lower proportion of accounting doctoral students indicate that their program requires*

Advances in Accounting Education: Teaching and Curriculum Innovations, Volume 18, 111–145
ISSN: 1085-4622/doi:10.1108/S1085-462220160000018005

proof of English proficiency prior to teaching, and pedagogical mentoring is rare across disciplines. Accounting and management doctoral students feel more prepared to teach undergraduate courses compared to finance and economics students. However, all disciplines indicate a relative lack of perceived preparation to teach graduate courses.

Practical implications − *This study provides empirical evidence of the current practices in pedagogical training of accounting, finance, management, and economics doctoral students.*

Social implications − *The results highlight several areas where accounting could possibly improve with regard to pedagogical training in doctoral programs. In particular we suggest (1) changes in the teaching evaluation process, (2) development of teaching mentorships, (3) implementing a teaching portfolio requirement, and (4) incorporation of additional methods of assisting non-native English speakers for teaching duties.*

Originality/value − *The study fills a gap in the literature regarding the pedagogical training in accounting doctoral programs.*

Keywords: Pedagogical training; doctoral programs

Although there is evidence that pedagogical training can improve the personal teaching efficacy of doctoral students (Burton, Bamberry, & Harris-Boundy, 2005), many students and recent graduates from doctoral programs in business do not feel adequately prepared to take on the responsibilities of teaching and maintaining a learning environment upon completion of their doctoral programs (Golde, 2004; Hershey, Vidyaranya, & Eatman, 1996; Utecht & Tullous, 2009). To better understand how accounting doctoral students are being prepared to assume the teaching responsibilities of faculty positions, this chapter examines current pedagogical training practices. We have three specific objectives with this study. First, we provide descriptive information about current practices in teaching preparation in U.S. accounting doctoral programs. Second, we collect and report comparative statistics from the related fields of finance, management, and economics for use as a benchmark. Finally, we provide suggestions and commentary about teaching preparation practices as revealed from the study.

Inarguably, the primary objective of Ph.D. programs in accounting and other business-related disciplines is to train students to become successful researchers. The emphasis on training Ph.D. students to be effective teachers, however, seems to differ within and across departments, colleges, and universities. There are many reasons why teaching effectiveness is worth consideration within Ph.D. programs. Adequate training for teaching not only prepares doctoral students to become effective teachers, but may also benefit research. Demski and Zimmerman (2000) argue that research and teaching are strong complements to each other and should not be separated. Further, being well prepared to teach is an asset to doctoral candidates entering the faculty job market (Backmon, 1998; Stammerjohan, Seifert, & Guidry, 2009).

Teaching and research expectations may vary greatly among different colleges and universities (Beyer, Herrmann, Meek, & Rapley, 2010), but teaching is the primary responsibility for most faculty members. In a recent survey of 16,112 full-time professors conducted by the Higher Education Research Institute, 74 percent report teaching as their principal activity and 97 percent view teaching as being "essential" or "very important" (Eagan et al., 2014). While some new faculty may receive positions where teaching responsibilities are limited, the majority of faculty positions require at least some evidence of high-quality teaching for promotion and tenure. Even if research is their primary focus, new faculty members will benefit from teaching preparation during their Ph.D. program as it will facilitate their ability to effectively manage their time concerning teaching and research responsibilities as they transition into their new faculty positions. Pedagogical training may be particularly relevant in accounting, as accounting academics appear to hold teaching as their primary interest more so than other academic disciplines (Hopwood, 2007).

We conduct a survey of the pedagogical training practices experienced by Ph.D. students in accounting, finance, management, and economics programs in the United States. Results indicate that accounting, finance, and management perform similarly with respect to providing doctoral students with first-hand teaching experience and requiring for-credit courses in teacher training. Accounting and management appear to utilize doctoral students as teaching assistants slightly less than the other disciplines we surveyed. When compared to the other disciplines, a lower proportion of accounting doctoral students indicate that their program requires additional proof of English proficiency, beyond program acceptance requirements, prior to teaching.[1] Furthermore, all four disciplines underutilize mentoring and peer reviews. With regard to doctoral student perceptions of teacher preparedness, we find that accounting and management doctoral students feel more prepared to teach undergraduate courses compared to finance and economics students. However, all disciplines indicate a relative lack of perceived preparation to teach graduate courses. Overall, respondents were neutral in their perceptions about how much importance their programs placed on preparing Ph.D. students to be effective teachers (neither important nor unimportant).

Specific to accounting, we find that participants from less prestigious doctoral programs feel more adequately prepared for undergraduate teaching duties than participants from more prestigious programs. We also find that, based on participant perceptions, less prestigious programs place greater importance on preparing doctoral students to be effective teachers than do more prestigious programs. In addition, doctoral students from less prestigious accounting programs indicated a greater number of courses taught and a greater number of course preparations compared to students from more prestigious programs, which may partially explain their perception of being more adequately prepared to teach.

This study makes several contributions to accounting education literature. First, we highlight areas where accounting could potentially improve with regard to pedagogical training and preparation in doctoral programs. For example, all of the disciplines we surveyed and particularly accounting could benefit from more extensive utilization of mentorship programs and peer reviews as part of teacher preparation and training procedures. Second, we highlight several areas where accounting seems to be leading or co-leading other similar disciplines with regard to teacher training and preparation. For instance, accounting and management appear to offer more direct, first-hand teaching experience than other disciplines. Finally, we document a wide range of perceptions on teaching and teacher preparation held by doctoral students. Responses indicate that while some students see great value in teaching, other students view it as a waste of time and resources. In summary, the information provided in this study may be a valuable resource for doctoral program directors, department chairs, deans, and other parties who may be interested in pedagogical training in doctoral programs.

BACKGROUND

Edwards, Ingram, and Sanders (1981) was one of the first studies to address the lack of attention given to teaching preparation in accounting doctoral programs. Their findings suggested that the majority of departmental administrators at that time believed that teaching skills and training received insufficient consideration in doctoral programs and thus recommended that academicians should place greater emphasis on cultivating teaching skills in doctoral programs. An Association to Advance Collegiate Schools of Business (AACSB) (1988) study further fueled the debate about the appropriate focus on teaching. This study suggested that the heavy focus on research resulted in business schools neglecting the application to practice (Utecht & Tullous, 2009). The lack of emphasis on teaching is not just specific to business schools. In a longitudinal study of graduate students across several disciplines, Austin (2002) finds that most participants did not feel prepared to take on the responsibilities of teaching and received insufficient guidance and training in many aspects of teaching.

Commissions have called for increased emphasis on teaching in accounting higher education.[2] For example, in 1990 the Accounting Education Change Commission (AECC) issued a statement recommending that "doctoral programs ... give more attention to teaching methods" (AECC, 1990, p. 310). More recently, the 2012 American Accounting Association (AAA) Pathways Commission expressed concerns about balancing all of the expectations for faculty given the heavy emphasis on research in the university culture. Further, their report recommended reformation in accounting education "so that teaching is respected and rewarded as a critical component in achieving each institution's mission" (Pathways Commission, 2012, p. 63). Similar to the AECC, the AAA Pathways Commission proposed several actions to achieve this reformation, including increasing the "reward, recognition, and support for high-quality teaching" and improving how "universities value the importance of teaching" (Pathways Commission, 2012, p. 12).

Accounting firms and organizations are actively involved in supporting doctoral education to ensure that there are an adequate number of professors to teach future accountants. For example, in 2008 the largest U.S. accounting firms and the American Institute of Certified Public Accountants (AICPA) Foundation created the Accounting Doctoral Scholars (ADS) Program. With the support of many of the largest accounting firms and 48 state CPA societies, the ADS program provided funding that allowed several accounting Ph.D. programs to admit additional students (ADS, 2013). Furthermore, Deloitte, Ernst & Young, KPMG, and PricewaterhouseCoopers established grants and scholarship programs to provide additional funding for doctoral study in accounting.

Research addressing pedagogical preparation in business doctoral programs provides some interesting insights into the role of teaching preparedness for future faculty. Although many business schools appear to be providing their doctoral students with some type of teaching experience prior to graduation, many students and recent graduates from doctoral programs in business do not feel adequately prepared for their post-graduation teaching responsibilities (Golde, 2004; Hershey et al., 1996). The majority of doctoral granting schools do not consider prospective students' teaching potential to be an important quality for admission into their programs (Behn, Carnes, Krull, Stocks, & Reckers, 2008). Despite this perception, many doctoral students view teaching as a stronger motivational factor than research (Plumlee, Kachelmeier, Madeo, Pratt, & Krull, 2006). Further, Gribbin, Sobery, and Braswell's (2002) study illustrates a gap between the amount of teaching training occurring in doctoral programs and departmental administrators' perceived importance of the role of teaching in hiring, promotion, and tenure decisions. Teaching quality also plays an important role in accreditation as the AACSB standards (2015) specifically highlight the importance of ensuring teaching that maximizes the potential for students to learn. Despite the growing awareness of the importance of teaching to the accounting profession and the desire for better teaching preparedness, there is very little evidence available to determine the extent to which accounting Ph.D. programs are effectively preparing students to become teachers or how accounting programs compare to other disciplines.

METHODOLOGY

The data collection process involved a three-step procedure. First, using the *2012 Hasselback Accounting Directory* (Hasselback, 2012), Brink, Glasscock, and Wier (2012), and an internet search, we identified 93 universities with active accounting doctoral programs in the United States (see Table 1).[3] Next, we accessed the websites for each of the 93 universities in an effort to locate information on teaching requirements, teaching-related training and mentoring activities, and other aspects of pedagogical focus within Ph.D. programs. For each of the 93 universities, we analyzed the doctoral program websites for the fields of accounting, finance, management, and economics.[4]

Table 1. Ph.D. Programs and Number of Student Survey Responses by Discipline.[a]

University	Accounting	Finance	Management	Economics[b]	Total
Arizona State University	2	NC	1	1*	4
Baruch College, CUNY	1	2	3	NP*	6
Bentley University	1	NP	2	NP	3
Boston University	NC	NC	NC	NC	0
Carnegie Mellon University	NC	0	1	3*	4
Case Western Reserve University	NC	NP	NC	NP	0
Columbia University	2	2	4	13	21
Cornell University	0	0	0	14	14
Drexel University	3	0	4	1*	8
Duke University	2	1	2	14	19
Emory University	1	0	0	2	3
Florida Atlantic University	NC	NC	NC	NP	0
Florida International University	NC	NC	NC	NC	0
Florida State University	7	0	4	1	12
The George Washington University	NC	NC	NC	3	3
Georgia Institute of Technology	3	0	4	0	7
Georgia State University	2	1	NC	3	6
Harvard University	NC	NC	NC	NC	0
Indiana University, Bloomington	4	1	4	NC	9
Jackson State University	NC	NC	NC	NC*	0
Kent State University	1	3	1	NP*	5
Louisiana State University	2	4	1	3*	10
Louisiana Tech University	NC	NC	NC	NC*	0
Massachusetts Institute of Technology	0	1	1	NC	2
Michigan State University	6	2	6	1	15
Mississippi State University	NC	NC	NC	NC*	0
Morgan State University	NC	NC	NC	NP	0
New York University	2	2	4	1	9
Northwestern University	2	4	3	4	13
The Ohio State University	3	0	2	NP	5
Oklahoma State University	2	3	4	0*	9
Pennsylvania State University	1	2	2	2	7
Purdue University	1	0	1	4*	6
Rutgers, The State University of New Jersey	7	2	2	1	12
Southern Illinois University	1	2	3	NC	6
Stanford University	0	0	0	0*	0
The State University of New York (SUNY), Binghamton	1	0	1	NC	2
SUNY, Buffalo	0	2	0	NC	2
Syracuse University	2	1	0	1	4
Temple University	1	0	0	2	3

Table 1. (*Continued*)

University	Accounting	Finance	Management	Economics[b]	Total
Texas A&M University, College Station	0	0	0	6	6
Texas Tech University	0	0	4	1	5
The University of Alabama	3	NC	6	NC*	9
University of Arkansas	5	1	2	0*	8
The University of Arizona	3	1	1	6*	11
University of California, Berkeley	0	1	0	9	10
University of California, Irvine	1	0	2	12	15
University of California, Los Angeles	1	0	0	10	11
University of Central Florida	6	3	3	NP*	12
The University of Chicago	1	1	0	4	6
University of Cincinnati	NC	0	0	0*	0
University of Colorado, Boulder	3	1	2	8	14
University of Connecticut	2	4	4	7	17
University of Florida	4	2	0	6*	12
University of Georgia	3	0	3	4*	10
University of Hawaii	0	NC	NC	NC	0
University of Houston	3	2	2	5	12
University of Illinois at Urbana Champaign	NC	0	NC	NC	0
The University of Iowa	3	0	5	4*	12
The University of Kansas	NC	NC	NC	NC	0
University of Kentucky	3	1	3	7*	14
The University of Maryland	2	1	0	12	15
University of Massachusetts	3	2	1	NC	6
The University of Memphis	NC	NC	NC	NC*	0
University of Miami	NC	NC	NC	NC*	0
University of Michigan	3	1	2	0	6
University of Minnesota	0	0	4	14	18
University of Mississippi	5	NC	NC	NC	5
University of Missouri	3	1	0	5	9
The University of Nebraska	0	0	0	3*	3
The University of North Carolina at Chapel Hill	2	2	4	2	10
University of North Texas	1	4	3	NP	8
University of Oklahoma	NC	2	0	0	2
University of Oregon	3	2	1	14	20
University of Pennsylvania	1	3	8	16	28
University of Pittsburgh	4	1	0	11	16
University of Rochester	0	0	1	6	7
University of South Carolina	6	2	2	1*	11
The University of South Florida	3	2	NP	3	8
University of Southern California	3	1	3	7	14

Table 1. (*Continued*)

University	Accounting	Finance	Management	Economics[b]	Total
The University of Tennessee	1	0	1	6*	8
The University of Texas, Arlington	NC	NC	NC	NP*	0
The University of Texas, Austin	0	3	3	10	16
The University of Texas, Dallas	3	1	5	NC	9
The University of Texas, El Paso	0	1	5	NP*	6
The University of Texas, San Antonio	2	1	0	NP*	3
The University of Utah	2	2	4	7	15
University of Washington	5	1	2	12	20
University of Wisconsin, Madison	4	0	2	19	25
Virginia Commonwealth University	8	NP	1	NP*	9
Virginia Tech	14	1	2	6	23
Washington State University	1	2	5	5	13
Washington University in St. Louis	1	2	3	0*	6
Yale University	NC	NC	NC	NC	0
Anonymous	2	0	0	1	3
Total institutions	*93*	*93*	*93*	*93*	*93*
Total survey responses	*183*	*90*	*159*	*323*	*755*
Programs represented by responses	*62*	*49*	*56*	*52*	*219*

[a]The following codes are used: NC = No contact for Ph.D. students was available on the university website; NP = No program was indicated in the field on the university website.
[b]Economics programs located within business schools are indicated with an asterisk (*).

We selected finance, management, and economics as similar fields for comparison because these fields share similarities in research and, therefore, will share many similarities in the content and structure of their Ph.D. programs. Specifically, there are abundant similarities and topical overlaps in the archival, analytic, behavioral, experimental, and theoretical research conducted in all four disciplines. However, we note that economics may differ from the other fields in several ways. First, economics is not always part of the business school as are the other fields. Thirty of the economics departments in the 93 universities examined in this study (32.26 percent) were in the business school. Second, economics Ph.D. programs tend to have higher admission and attrition rates than accounting, finance, or management (Stock, Finegan, & Siegfried, 2006; Stock, Siegfried, & Finegan, 2011). Specifically, we observed the following mean (median) program sizes based on the website student listings: accounting 7.47 (9) students, ranging from 1 to 34, finance 9.51 (9) students, ranging from 1 to 33, management 8.98 (8) students, ranging from 1 to 37, and economics 32.49 (17.5) students, ranging from 1 to 153.[5] Due to the number of students in economics

Ph.D. programs, it is less likely that all students will be given the opportunity to teach a course. Third, compared to the other disciplines, fewer economics doctoral students receive stipends. This could explain some variation in participant responses between disciplines.[6] Finally, the number of economics Ph.D. students pursuing careers outside of academia tends to be larger than that of the other fields in our study (Chen, Liu, & Billger, 2013). These differences should be kept in mind while interpreting our results.

We encountered tremendous variation in the level of detail, timeliness, and overall content of the website information. Some program websites reflect recent updates and contain extensive information regarding teaching-related requirements and activities. Other websites appear to have not been updated for several years and/or make virtually no mention of teaching-related program requirements or activities. Due to this wide variation, we were able to draw little inference into teaching preparation and requirements of the various doctoral programs from the website data.

The final step in the data collection process involved the development and distribution of a survey questionnaire to current Ph.D. students in accounting, finance, management, and economics programs in the universities identified above.[7] Prior to distributing the survey instrument, we conducted a pilot test with a small sample of Ph.D. students and made appropriate adjustments to the instrument based on the feedback from pilot test participants. The final questionnaire contained 37 questions with items inquiring about doctoral program teaching requirements, teaching-related training and mentoring activities, feedback on teaching, and participant background/demographic information. A well-known online service provider administered the survey. Upon survey completion, participants could enter into a drawing to win one of four $50 Amazon gift cards. The online survey service administered the drawing. On average, participants took approximately 10 minutes to complete the survey.

When available, we gathered doctoral student names and email addresses from the respective universities' departmental websites. In this way, we identified 4,984 potential survey respondents (711 in accounting, 852 in finance, 826 in management, and 2,595 in economics). We then emailed these contacts an invitation to participate in our survey, along with a link to the survey. Table 1 displays survey responses by university and discipline. It is important to note that not all universities have programs in all disciplines. For example, a university may have doctoral programs in accounting, management, and finance but not economics. When a Ph.D. program in a specific discipline is not offered, the table indicates no

Table 2. Ph.D. Student Response Rates.

	Accounting	Finance	Management	Economics	Total
Denominator					
Total email addresses	711	852	826	2,595	4,984
Less: Unusable email addresses	23	15	18	43	99
Total viable emails	688	837	808	2,552	4,885
Numerator					
Student responses from original population	184	90	159	324	757
Less: Unusable response	1	0	0	1	2
Total usable responses	183	90	159	323	755
Ph.D. student response rate	26.6%	10.8%	19.7%	12.7%	15.5%
Career orientation					
Academia and undecided	183	86	158	294	722
Non-academia	0	4	1	29	33

program, "NP." Further, we were unable to locate Ph.D. student contact information for some programs. When Ph.D. student contact information was unavailable, this is indicated in the table with the code for no contact available, "NC." As shown in Table 1, 62 out of 93 accounting programs (66.7 percent) are represented with at least one survey response.

Table 2 provides information on survey response rates. In total, we sent 4,984 emails to potential participants. Ninety-nine emails were returned as unusable, resulting in 4,885 valid emails. We obtained 755 survey responses, representing a total response rate of 15.5 percent. By discipline, response rates ranged from 10.8 percent (finance) to 26.6 percent (accounting). Given that our online survey was anonymous, the likelihood of response bias (i.e., social desirability bias, demand effects, acquiescence bias) is low.

RESULTS

We present results in the following order. First, we provide the demographic information for the doctoral students who participated in the survey. Then we discuss responses across each discipline regarding: (1) teaching responsibilities, (2) teaching preparation and training, and (3) perceptions on teaching preparedness in the doctoral program. Lastly, we discuss the results of additional analyses.

Demographics of Doctoral Students

We collected responses from 755 doctoral students enrolled in Ph.D. programs in accounting, finance, management, or economics. The majority of respondents, 448 (59.30 percent), are male, and 215 respondents (28.50 percent) are international students. The average respondent age is 30 years (ranging from 21 to 61 years). The majority of respondents across disciplines indicate their intention to pursue a career in academia (see Table 3). In order to provide meaningful comparisons across disciplines, all analyses subsequent to demographic information include only respondents who indicated plans to pursue a career in academia or were undecided about career plans. Respondents who indicated non-academia career plans were dropped from further analyses.

Educational History and Teaching Experience

We ask participants to list the academic degrees they earned prior to entering their Ph.D. programs. With the exception of economics, responses indicate that the majority of doctoral students across disciplines attained a Master's degree prior enrolling in their Ph.D. program (75.96 percent of accounting

Table 3. Characteristics of Doctoral Students by Discipline.

	Frequency			
	Accounting ($n = 183$)	Finance ($n = 90$)	Management ($n = 159$)	Economics ($n = 323$)
Age (mean)	31	31	32	27
Gender (male)	56.30%	71.10%	51.60%	61.60%
International students	13.70%	42.20%	25.20%	34.70%
Prior Master's degree	75.96%	65.56%	71.07%	36.22%
Prior Doctorate degree	0.55%	3.33%	2.52%	0.31%
Prior teaching experience				
Any prior teaching experience	46.99%	48.89%	50.94%	39.94%
Undergraduate – freshman/ sophomore level courses	24.04%	23.33%	23.27%	26.63%
Undergraduate – junior/senior level courses	13.66%	21.11%	14.47%	17.03%
Graduate-level courses	10.38%	10.00%	5.66%	5.57%
Non-academic/professional development courses	16.94%	15.56%	23.90%	5.57%
Other (e.g., high school)	34.97%	31.11%	26.42%	30.03%
In the same discipline as Ph.D.	36.61%	26.67%	18.24%	26.63%

students, 65.56 percent of finance students, 71.07 percent of management students, and 36.22 percent of economics students). Interestingly, almost half (45 percent) of the total respondents specify that they had teaching experience before starting their Ph.D. program. We also ask participants to indicate if their prior teaching experience was in the same field as their current Ph.D. program. Results show that 36.61 percent of accounting students, 26.67 percent of finance students, 18.24 percent of management students, and 26.63 percent of economics students indicated that they had teaching experience in the same field as their current Ph.D. discipline.

Teaching Responsibilities

In order to examine teaching responsibilities of doctoral students in each discipline, the survey asks respondents to indicate the appropriate teaching responsibilities and requirements that best describe their program. Table 4 presents the summary of teaching responsibilities in accounting, finance, management, and economics doctoral programs, respectively. We request that respondents indicate the teaching role(s) that students in their program assume (primary instructor or non-instructor teaching assistant), and then we inquire about the responsibilities for each role. These responses are aggregated by school so that each school is given an average, and then schools are equally weighted to provide an average for each discipline.[8]

Primary Instructor
Results show that 86.72 percent of accounting programs represented by our respondents have students teach at least one or more courses during the doctoral program, compared to 77.94 percent of finance programs, 87.84 percent of management programs, and 70.43 percent of economics programs. Further, just over 50 percent of accounting programs require teaching as a primary instructor for both graduation and basic funding, while 26.16 percent of accounting programs make teaching as a primary instructor optional for additional funding. Similar responses are obtained from management and finance. However, only 15.34 percent of economics programs require teaching as a primary instructor for graduation, while 31.64 percent indicate a requirement to teach for basic funding. In addition, 43.30 percent of economics programs make teaching as primary instructor optional for additional funding.

For programs with doctoral students that teach, 70.65 percent of accounting programs have students teach freshman/sophomore level courses, compared to only 48.98 percent of finance programs, 48.21 percent

Table 4. Ph.D. Programs Teaching Assignments.[a]

	Primary Instructor				Non-Instructor Teaching Assistant			
	Accounting (n = 62)	Finance (n = 49)	Management (n = 56)	Economics (n = 52)	Accounting (n = 62)	Finance (n = 49)	Management (n = 56)	Economics (n = 52)
Program requirement								
Required for graduation	50.84%	44.56%	54.82%	15.34%	22.40%	18.03%	24.72%	16.40%
Required for basic funding	52.47%	34.52%	50.15%	31.64%	52.02%	53.23%	49.67%	72.16%
Optional for additional funding	26.16%	24.83%	27.90%	43.30%	19.54%	12.93%	24.45%	19.05%
Not applicable	7.58%	9.01%	3.50%	8.93%	14.99%	9.69%	12.98%	2.74%
Assignment level								
Undergraduate – freshman/sophomore level courses	70.65%	48.98%	48.21%	61.54%	27.74%	24.66%	21.65%	51.78%
Undergraduate – junior/senior level courses	59.73%	58.33%	78.96%	48.37%	26.42%	39.80%	25.55%	53.01%
Graduate-level courses	10.00%	5.27%	9.70%	8.66%	34.39%	50.85%	42.86%	55.50%
Primary instructor assignments								
Course preparations (mean)	1.54	1.64	1.65	1.79				
Percentage of doctoral students who teach during program	86.72%	77.94%	87.84%	70.43%				
Non-instructor responsibilities								
Grading					65.06%	71.26%	63.62%	82.89%
Leading lab or study sessions					35.53%	37.76%	33.13%	61.03%
Tutoring during office hours					42.80%	56.80%	33.38%	72.72%

[a]The information in this table reflects unweighted averages reported by discipline. Each school contributes equal weighting to the reported discipline averages. Thus, the weight placed on schools with multiple respondents is equal to the weight placed on schools with one respondent.

of management programs, and 61.54 percent of economics programs. Relative to management programs, accounting, finance, and economics students have less experience teaching junior/senior level courses. Specifically, 59.73 percent of accounting programs, 58.33 percent of finance programs, 78.96 percent of management programs, and 48.37 percent of economics programs have doctoral students as a primary instructor in undergraduate junior/senior level courses. The percentage of doctoral programs that have doctoral students teach graduate-level courses is quite low, ranging from 5.27 percent to 10.00 percent across the four disciplines.

Across all disciplines, the average number of course preparations is quite similar.[9] Average course preparations for students in accounting, finance, management, and economics over the duration of the program are 1.54, 1.64, 1.65, and 1.79, respectively. Table 5 reports the percentage of students teaching as a primary instructor during the Ph.D. program based on students' annual teaching loads for each discipline. In accounting, most teaching occurs during the third and fourth years. Reported teaching assignments are similar in the other disciplines. Unlike the other disciplines, the majority of students in economics programs report that they have a zero teaching load as a primary instructor during the program (untabulated).

Non-Instructor Teaching Assistant
Doctoral students may also be involved in the teaching process as non-instructor teaching assistants. The majority of respondents across all

Table 5. Primary Instructor Teaching Responsibilities by Year.[a]

	Percentage of Students Teaching During the Ph.D. Program					
	1st year (%)	2nd year (%)	3rd year (%)	4th year (%)	5th year (%)	Additional years (%)
Accounting doctoral programs (n = 62)	7.95	11.98	18.60	16.19	9.64	4.39
Finance doctoral programs (n = 49)	2.41	8.08	15.96	18.45	15.56	8.48
Management doctoral programs (n = 56)	4.08	11.47	19.71	19.44	12.86	7.65
Economics doctoral programs (n = 52)	3.59	10.82	17.47	17.66	11.92	7.09

[a]The information in this table reflects unweighted averages reported by discipline. Each school contributes equal weighting to the reported discipline averages. Thus, the weight placed on schools with multiple respondents is equal to the weight placed on schools with one respondent.

disciplines indicate that being a teaching assistant is required for basic funding. The reported teaching assistant assignments are generally similar across the disciplines, except economics. As reported in Table 4, respondents in economics programs indicate a much heavier teaching assistantship load than the other three disciplines. For example, 27.74 percent of accounting programs, 24.66 percent of finance programs, and 21.65 percent of management programs have students who indicate they work as teaching assistants in undergraduate freshmen/sophomore level courses, compared to 51.78 percent of economics programs. Results are similar for teaching assistant expectations for junior/senior level courses and graduate-level courses, with one notable exception. In the finance discipline, teaching assistant expectations in graduate courses rise to levels comparable to economics. In sum, it appears that accounting and management doctoral programs require slightly less teaching assistantship-related responsibilities compared to the other disciplines.

We also ask respondents to indicate the types of responsibilities that are required as teaching assistants. The data indicate a consistent trend across all disciplines. Grading is the first responsibility, followed by tutoring during office hours, and leading lab or study sessions. Some respondents also identify other forms of teaching assistant responsibilities, including proctoring exams, preparing teaching materials (i.e., homework, quizzes, solutions, or problem sets), substituting for the primary instructor, and performing administrative tasks (i.e., maintaining learning websites, answering emails, and taking class attendance).

Teaching Preparation

Teaching Training
We ask respondents to provide information about the training they typically receive during their doctoral programs related to teaching. We inquire about both required and elective training, as well as various formats of training (i.e., courses for credit, courses not for credit, workshops, and mentoring). Responses pertaining to doctoral students' teaching preparation and training are presented in Table 6. We find that 31.07 percent of accounting programs require a for-credit course, compared to 29.76 percent of finance programs, 33.13 percent of management programs, and 21.22 percent of economics programs.

Results regarding the prevalence of other formats of teacher training are mixed. Across disciplines, the prevalence of elective, for-credit courses

Table 6. Ph.D. Program Formal Teaching Training.[a]

	Accounting (n = 62) (%)	Finance (n = 49) (%)	Management (n = 56) (%)	Economics (n = 52) (%)
Courses for credit				
Required	31.07	29.76	33.13	21.22
Elective	11.03	4.08	11.79	7.38
Workshops (not for credit)				
Required	25.23	27.72	36.79	36.43
Elective	22.38	25.51	30.28	21.09
Mentoring program				
Required	5.97	10.88	5.68	6.60
Elective	6.60	6.80	18.91	5.92
Other training/requirements				
Additional proof of English proficiency prior to teaching for students whose native language is not English	21.46	44.22	26.29	51.92
Required to develop a teaching portfolio	11.84	15.82	26.67	17.42
Receive guidance for solving ethical violations in the classroom	55.09	49.49	60.03	60.62

[a]The information in this table reflects unweighted averages reported by discipline. Each school contributes equal weighting to the reported discipline averages. Thus, the weight placed on schools with multiple respondents is equal to the weight placed on schools with one respondent.

ranges from 4.08 percent to 11.79 percent of programs. Economics and management lead the other disciplines in the percentage of programs requiring a not-for-credit course or workshop on teacher training, while management programs are the most likely to have an elective, not-for-credit course or workshop on teacher training. Mentorship is not actively utilized as a tool for teacher training and preparation in most of the doctoral programs we examine. Results show that only 12.57 percent of accounting, 17.68 percent of finance, 24.59 percent of management, and 12.52 percent of economics programs either require a mentorship or make it available as an elective training tool.

English Proficiency

English proficiency standardized tests (i.e., Test of English as a Foreign Language (TOEFL) and/or International English Language Testing System (IELTS) tests) are typically compulsory as part of a doctoral program's admission requirements for international applicants for whom

English is not their native language. We ask participants if their program requires students whose first language is not English to demonstrate additional proof of English proficiency beyond that of standardized testing prior to teaching. Reponses (see Table 6) indicate that 21.46 percent of accounting programs require additional proof of English proficiency prior to teaching, compared to 44.22 percent for finance, 26.29 percent for management, and 51.92 percent for economics. However, it should be noted that while accounting had the lowest percentage among all disciplines for required additional proof of English proficiency prior to teaching, it also had the lowest percentage of international student respondents.

Respondents further identify types of English proficiency improvement programs offered or required by their doctoral programs. Based on survey responses, common English proficiency improvement training programs are English as Second Language (ESL) courses, English presentation and speaking courses or tests, accent reduction courses, writing skills training, International Teaching Assistant (ITA) workshops, and mock teaching sessions. One illustrative response is as follows:

> I believe the school offers a mentor, requires additional English proficiency testing, and additional teaching workshops geared towards overcoming cultural boundaries and teaching American students.

Teaching Portfolio

Teaching portfolios can be useful to document and depict an individual's capability and performance in teaching, and they are a beneficial tool for developing teaching abilities and fostering the scholarship of teaching (Babin, Shaffer, & Tomas, 2002; Calegari, Geisler, & Larkins, 1999; Stewart, 2004). Based on our survey, it appears few programs require doctoral students to develop a teaching portfolio across disciplines. Respondents indicate that only 11.84 percent of accounting programs require students to develop a teaching portfolio (see Table 6). The percentages are also relatively low for the other disciplines, with 15.82 percent for finance, 26.67 percent for management, and 17.42 percent for economics.

Ethical Violations

Instructors may encounter ethical violations in the classroom, and universities often have policies and procedures in place to handle such violations. For example, there may be a predetermined course of action instructors are expected to take when documenting a cheating incident. We examine the extent to which doctoral programs provide guidance for solving ethical violations and find that many respondents across disciplines report that they do receive formal training on how to deal with possible ethical violations in the classroom. Specifically, respondents in 55.09 percent of accounting programs reported that they receive such guidance. Other disciplines reported similar levels of training on average (see Table 6).

Teaching Feedback

Table 7 reports results of items relating to feedback doctoral students receive on their teaching. The survey inquired about several types of teaching-related feedback, including student evaluations, peer reviews, and teaching awards. Not surprisingly, a majority of respondents across disciplines report that their programs actively use student evaluations to measure individuals' teaching performance. The data suggest that peer reviews are not widely

Table 7.   Ph.D. Program Teaching Feedback.[a]

	Accounting ($n = 62$) (%)	Finance ($n = 49$) (%)	Management ($n = 56$) (%)	Economics ($n = 52$) (%)
Student evaluations are actively used to gauge teaching performance in the program	66.62	53.91	65.94	48.44
Teaching awards are offered	47.66	47.11	50.04	46.44
Peer reviews in teaching				
By other Ph.D. students	2.96	0.51	2.14	4.07
By faculty members	10.22	11.90	17.29	12.83
No, peer reviews are not required	74.89	68.71	70.30	61.38
Repercussions for poor Ph.D. student teaching performance				
Reprimanded by department chair or other superior	13.93	8.84	14.54	13.92
Required to receive additional training on teaching	11.31	11.73	11.19	10.25
Reduced teaching load	7.12	10.03	6.43	14.11
Removed from the program	0.12	1.19	1.49	0.96
Don't know	68.83	53.57	61.49	48.31
Have you ever witnessed a student being reprimanded for a teaching-related failure?	7.02	8.84	5.63	8.27

[a]The information in this table reflects unweighted averages reported by discipline. Each school contributes equal weighting to the reported discipline averages. Thus, the weight placed on schools with multiple respondents is equal to the weight placed on schools with one respondent.

utilized as a teaching performance feedback tool in doctoral programs. Peer reviews seem to be least utilized in accounting, as 74.89 percent of programs do not require peer reviews. Furthermore, peer reviews are conducted by fellow doctoral students in only 2.96 percent of accounting programs, and peer reviews are conducted by faculty members in 10.22 percent of accounting programs.

We also examine the usage of teaching awards as a feedback mechanism. Teaching awards can be utilized to recognize and reward good teaching and may also encourage and promote a high level of teaching performance (Chism & Szabo, 1997). Survey responses reflect little variation across disciplines, with responses indicating that approximately half of programs offer some type of teaching awards (see Table 7). Participants further described the teaching awards available in their programs in an open-response question. Descriptions indicate that awards range from simple recognitions from the school to cash awards. We also find that teaching award implementation procedures vary broadly. Some programs grant awards based solely on teaching performance as reflected by student evaluations. In contrast, other programs have extensive award procedures, as described by one of our accounting respondents as follows:

> An award is given every semester to one outstanding Ph.D. student. The student must submit a packet including course syllabus, description of teaching philosophy, and an example of a course material (quiz, etc.) created by the student (and a letter of recommendation by the primary instructor if the student is acting as a TA). A committee of faculty, Ph.D. students, and undergraduates then review the packet, observe the candidate in the classroom, and review student evaluations in determining the recipient.

Finally, we investigate whether doctoral students face ramifications for poor teaching performance. We inquire about several potential consequences doctoral students may face, including being reprimanded, requirements to take additional teaching-related training, teaching load reduction, or removal from the program. Interestingly, the majority of respondents across disciplines report that they do not know whether there are repercussions for poor teaching performance. Respondents in 13.93 percent of accounting programs indicate that students will be reprimanded as a consequence for poor teaching performance. Furthermore, respondents in 11.31 percent of accounting programs indicate that their program requires students to receive additional teaching-related training if teaching performance is poor. As shown in Table 7, results are similar across all disciplines. Several open-response comments on this matter explain that poor teaching performance may cause economic repercussions, as students' funding may be reduced or rescinded. Further, the open-response comments highlight students' confusion as to what repercussions, if any, occur for poor teaching performance, and several comments highlighted students' perceptions that the quality of teaching was of little importance in their program.

Doctoral Students' Perceptions of Teaching Preparation

To examine doctoral student perceptions of teaching preparedness in their programs, we ask respondents three questions (see Table 8). First, we ask respondents to indicate their level of agreement with the following statement: "I feel like the training and experience my program offers will adequately prepare me for teaching undergraduate courses." The second statement is identical, with the substitution of graduate rather than undergraduate courses. Respondents provide answers on a 7-point Likert scale ranging from 1 ("strongly disagree") to 7 ("strongly agree").

For the first item, mean responses indicate that accounting and management doctoral students feel more adequately prepared to teach undergraduate courses compared to finance and economics doctoral students. The mean responses for accounting and management are virtually identical at 5.47 and 5.48, respectively, while mean responses for finance and economics are lower at 5.15 and 5.28, respectively. While an ANOVA does not indicate a significant effect of discipline ($F = 1.066$, $p = 0.363$), the difference between these two groups (accounting/management and finance/economics) is significant at the .10 level ($t = 1.693$, $p = 0.091$). Overall, respondents indicate slight agreement with the statement that their doctoral programs offer adequate training and experience to prepare them for undergraduate teaching assignments.

Respondents across all disciplines indicate a neutral response to the statement that their doctoral programs adequately prepare them to teach graduate-level courses. The mean responses from accounting, finance, management, and economics students are 4.60, 4.67, 4.47, and 4.62, respectively. We find no significant mean differences across the disciplines ($F = 0.319$, $p = 0.812$).

Third, we ask each respondent to indicate how much importance their program places on preparing Ph.D. students to be effective teachers. Participants respond using a 7-point Likert-type scale ranging from 1 ("very unimportant") to 7 ("very important"). Interestingly, we find that on average, respondents across all disciplines perceive that their program views preparing doctoral students to be effective teachers as neither

Table 8. Doctoral Students' Perceptions on Teaching Preparation in the Ph.D. Program.

	Accounting (n = 183)		Finance (n = 90)		Management (n = 159)		Economics (n = 323)	
	Mean	s.d.	Mean	s.d.	Mean	s.d.	Mean	s.d.
I feel like the training and experience my program offers will adequately prepare me for teaching *undergraduate* courses.[a]	5.47	1.66	5.15	1.86	5.48	1.57	5.28	1.66
I feel like the training and experience my program offers will adequately prepare me for teaching *graduate* courses.[a]	4.60	1.75	4.67	1.90	4.47	1.68	4.62	1.70
Indicate how much importance your Ph.D. program places on preparing Ph.D. students to be effective teachers.[b]	4.52	1.54	4.24	1.73	4.40	1.68	4.14	1.74

[a]Measured on a 7-point Likert scale where 1 = "Strongly Disagree," 4 = "Neither Agree nor Disagree," and 7 = "Strongly Agree."
[b]Measured on a 7-point Likert scale where 1 = "Very Unimportant," 4 = "Neither Important nor Unimportant," and 7 = "Very Important."

important nor unimportant (all means were near the midpoint of 4 on the scale). The mean responses from accounting, finance, management, and economics students are 4.52, 4.24, 4.40, and 4.14, respectively. Tests for mean differences indicate differences across programs ($F = 1.719$, $p = 0.076$). Specifically, Tukey's least significant difference (results untabulated) show that the mean for economics is statistically different from the other three disciplines.[10]

Helpful Teaching Preparation Tools

Using an open-response question, we ask respondents to identify the most helpful teaching preparation tools they have encountered during their doctoral programs. A total of 301 participants provide responses. Respondents indicate that the most helpful teacher training practice is teaching experience and/or being a primary instructor (28.57 percent). The majority of these respondents note that although teaching-related courses or workshops are beneficial, the opportunity to actually teach helps them shape and improve their teaching skills. One respondent explained that the actual experience of being an instructor allowed him or her to "understand how to teach to a variety of students, deal with common questions and concerns of students, and how to balance courses or research load while teaching." In addition, eight percent of respondents laud the benefits of working as a teaching assistant. They note that teaching assistantships can act as a beneficial stepping-stone to obtaining the required skills needed for teaching.

Mentorships (by faculty members or senior cohorts) rank as the second most useful teaching tool as identified by respondents (21.59 percent). Mentors can provide active discussion and advice regarding best practices and teaching materials and can provide constructive feedback. One respondent explains:

> Once a professor visited my class and gave me feedback on what I could improve. This was especially helpful since his advice was specific. I feel that many teaching prep advice just stays in useless generalities (e.g., "a good teacher respects and engages the students." I could have figured that one out myself; no need for a training program to tell me that). To be useful, teacher preparation must be specific and go beyond the obvious.

The third and fourth most popular teaching preparation tools identified by respondents include attending teaching-related courses, workshops, and other training (14.95 percent), and observing faculty members or senior cohort members in the classroom (5.64 percent). As noted by some respondents, shadowing other instructors allows doctoral students to obtain a realistic view of how to conduct a classroom. Other beneficial teaching preparation tools mentioned by respondents include practicing and recording teaching sessions; developing communication, presentation, and time management skills; working closely with fellow doctoral students; mastering the learning support technology (i.e., Blackboard and Canvas); and improving English skills. Nine percent of the 301 respondents indicate they have not received any useful teaching training from their programs. Of this nine percent who indicate no useful teaching training, most (77 percent) had experience as a primary instructor.

Additional Analyses

Proportion of Negative Open-Response Comments
We also examine whether the proportion of negative open-response comments regarding teaching differs among accounting, finance, management, and economics students. We define "negative comments" as any in which the participant either expressed a personal negative view about teaching or exposed a negative perception of teaching by their program. We identified 22 negative open-response comments and computed negative comment rates for each discipline and compared these to the overall proportion of responses by discipline (untabulated). Results indicate a relatively low number of negative open-response comments from accounting participants. Specifically, only nine percent of the negative comments came from accounting participants, while accounting comprised 24 percent of total survey responses. Conversely, management participants provided a higher rate of negative open-response comments. Forty-one percent of negative comments came from management participants, while management comprised only 21 percent of total survey responses. Negative comment response rates for finance and economics were more in line with their respective proportions of survey responses. Specifically, finance accounted for 18 percent of negative comments while comprising 12 percent of total survey responses; economics accounted for 32 percent of negative comments while comprising 43 percent of total survey responses.

Accounting Responses Partitioned by School Prestige
We examine whether accounting participant views on certain teaching and teaching preparation items differ by the prestige of doctoral institutions. Using the prestige rankings from Fogarty and Markarian (2007), we separate our sample into quartiles based on program prestige (see Fogarty & Markarian, 2007, for the ranking and quartiles). By necessity, we omitted

participant responses from schools not in the Fogarty and Markarian (2007) ranking, which resulted in 22 dropped responses. Results are shown in Table 9.

Using this partitioned data, we first examine responses to the following survey question: "If you plan to pursue a job in academia, what relative weight do you hope to have allocated to research, teaching, and service?" We report the percentages for teaching. As shown in Table 9, Panel A, participants from schools in quartile 1 (most prestigious) desire that 28.73 percent of their workload be comprised of teaching. In contrast, participants from schools in quartile 4 (least prestigious) desire that 40.03 percent of their workload be teaching. This difference is statistically significant ($p = 0.004$). The differences in the percentages for research and teaching between the 4 quartiles are not statistically significant (untabulated). For all 4 quartiles, the relative weight allocated to teaching was less than the weight allocated to research. Thus, the anticipated allocation of time to teaching is less than research for students from all institutions regardless of prestige. This finding is surprising in light of the Higher Education Research Institute's survey where the majority of respondents (full-time professors) indicated that teaching was their principle activity (Eagan et al., 2014).

Next we examine responses to the following survey item: "Please indicate your level of agreement with this statement: I feel like the training and experience my program offers will adequately prepare me for teaching undergraduate courses." Responses were provided on a 7-point Likert scale. As shown in Table 9, Panel B, participants from quartile 1 (most prestigious) schools indicate significantly less agreement to this statement (mean = 4.81) than participants from quartile 4 (least prestigious) schools (mean = 5.88, $p = 0.053$). Thus, it appears that participants from less prestigious schools feel more adequately prepared for undergraduate teaching duties than participants from more prestigious schools.

We also examine responses to the following survey item: "On the scale below, please indicate how much importance your Ph.D. program places on preparing Ph.D. students to be effective teachers." Responses were provided on a 7-point Likert scale. As shown in Table 9, Panel B, participants from quartile 1 (most prestigious) schools indicate significantly less importance placed on teaching preparation and effectiveness (mean = 3.69) than participants from quartile 4 (least prestigious) schools (mean = 4.61, $p = 0.070$). Participants from quartile 3 schools indicate the highest importance placed on teaching preparation and effectiveness (mean = 4.83).

Finally, we examine whether students from less prestigious accounting doctoral programs actually teach more than students from more prestigious

Table 9.   Doctoral Students' Perceptions on Teaching Preparation by School Prestige.

	First Quartile (Most Prestigious) (n = 13)		Second Quartile (n = 16)		Third Quartile (n = 12)		Fourth Quartile (Least Prestigious) (n = 11)	
	Mean	s.d.	Mean	s.d.	Mean	s.d.	Mean	s.d.
Panel A: Mean relative weight in teaching[a]								
If you plan to pursue a job in academia, what relative weight do you hope to have allocated to teaching over research and service?[b]	28.73%	7.46	32.04%	6.21	35.32%	8.73	40.03%	8.68

	First Quartile (Most Prestigious) (n = 32)		Second Quartile (n = 40)		Third Quartile (n = 46)		Fourth Quartile (Least Prestigious) (n = 33)	
	Mean	s.d.	Mean	s.d.	Mean	s.d.	Mean	s.d.
Panel B: Doctoral students' perceptions on teaching preparation in Ph.D. program								
I feel like the training and experience my program offers will adequately prepare me for teaching *undergraduate* courses.[c]	4.81	2.11	5.53	1.41	5.54	1.63	5.88	1.41
As primary instructor, how many courses with substantially different content will you prepare and teach during your Ph.D. program?	1.12	0.97	1.38	0.69	2.21	1.07	1.76	0.98
Indicate how much importance your Ph.D. program places on preparing Ph.D. students to be effective teachers.[d]	3.69	1.59	4.53	1.37	4.83	1.61	4.61	1.39

[a]The information in this table reflects unweighted averages reported by discipline. Each school contributes equal weighting to the reported discipline averages. Thus, the weight placed on schools with multiple respondents is equal to the weight placed on schools with one respondent.
[b]Measured as a number between 0 and 100, and all three answers among research, teaching, and service will add up to 100.
[c]Measured on a 7-point Likert scale where 1 = "Strongly Disagree," 4 = "Neither Agree nor Disagree," and 7 = "Strongly Agree."
[d]Measured on a 7-point Likert scale where 1 = "Very Unimportant," 4 = "Neither Important nor Unimportant," and 7 = "Very Important."

programs. We asked participants, "As primary instructor, how many courses with substantially different content will you prepare and teach during your Ph.D. program?" As shown in Table 9, Panel B, participants from quartile 1 (most prestigious) schools indicate significantly fewer course preparations (mean = 1.12) than participants from quartile 4 (least prestigious) schools (mean = 1.76, $p = 0.033$). Students from quartile 3 (less prestigious) indicated the highest mean number of course preparations at 2.21.

Most accounting doctoral students indicate that they begin teaching during the third year of the Ph.D. program. In a supplemental analysis (untabulated), we analyze the number of classes for which students are the primary instructor during the third year of the Ph.D. program. Consistent with the previous analysis, results indicate that doctoral students from less prestigious programs teach more than doctoral students from more prestigious programs. Specifically, participants from quartile 1 (most prestigious) schools indicate significantly fewer courses taught during the third year (mean = 0.68) compared to participants from quartile 4 (least prestigious) schools (mean = 2.29, $p < 0.001$). Interestingly, but still in line with the main findings, participants from quartile 2 schools (more prestigious) indicate the fewest number of courses taught (mean = 0.32) while participants from quartile 3 schools (less prestigious) indicate the greatest number of courses taught (2.90). This difference is also statistically significant ($p < 0.001$). In summary, it appears that students at less prestigious schools teach more during their Ph.D. programs and feel more prepared to teach than those who attend more prestigious Ph.D. programs.

DISCUSSION

The primary purpose of this study was to assess how well accounting doctoral students are being prepared to assume teaching responsibilities and to compare teaching preparedness in accounting doctoral programs to doctoral programs in similar disciplines. We collected survey responses from students in accounting, finance, management, and economics doctoral programs.

This study is descriptive in nature and therefore cannot yield inferences about the effectiveness of particular teacher preparation programs or a specific discipline's practice with regard to teacher training. Furthermore, we cannot use this data to make inferences about the value of teaching versus research. Instead, we can inform readers about the current pedagogical training practices in accounting doctoral programs as compared to programs in similar disciplines.

Given the caveat above, these results highlight several areas where accounting appears to compare favorably to the other disciplines and areas where accounting could potentially improve. For example, we find that accounting and management doctoral programs outperform other similar disciplines with respect to providing doctoral students with first-hand teaching experience and with offering required for-credit courses in teacher training. On the other hand, a lower percentage of accounting doctoral students indicate that their program requires additional proof of English proficiency, beyond program acceptance requirements, prior to allowing doctoral students to teach.[11] Across disciplines, results also indicate that mentoring programs and peer reviews are rarely utilized as methods of teaching preparation, particularly in accounting.

We also find that the doctoral students we surveyed, particularly in accounting and management, feel moderately prepared to teach undergraduate courses, but they feel less prepared to teach graduate courses. However, students' perceptions of the importance their Ph.D. programs place on teaching effectiveness and preparedness give some cause for concern. On average, respondents from all four disciplines indicate that their programs view teaching preparation as neither important nor unimportant. Thus, Ph.D. programs do not appear to be sending a consistent clear signal that teaching effectiveness is valuable.

With respect to accounting, we find that participants from less prestigious accounting doctoral programs feel more adequately prepared for undergraduate teaching duties than participants from more prestigious accounting programs. Participants also indicate that less prestigious accounting programs place greater importance on preparing doctoral students to be effective teachers than do more prestigious accounting programs. In addition, students from less prestigious programs teach more courses and have more course preparations than do students from more prestigious accounting programs.

The disparity in perceptions was also evident in students' responses to the open-response questions. While many students volunteered opinions that indicated that they felt teaching quality and preparation was important, almost as many unequivocally stated that teaching was of no importance to them or their program advisors. The following two quotes from accounting respondents illustrate the opposing views:

> From my perspective, teaching is an under-appreciated aspect of Ph.D. programs. While quality research and publications are important, all faculty will influence and interface with students who are trying to gain basic accounting knowledge and understand how they can fit into the profession. We can publish all the best research in the

world, but if we don't have quality professionals coming from our programs, our research may well be worthless.

I hate teaching. I entered wanting to teach as much as research, but now it's a thorn in my side.

Many of the respondents expressing negative viewpoints often reference the relative importance of teaching to research. The following comments illustrate these opinions:

My school, like so many others, considers teaching to be unimportant. You don't need a survey to learn this.

Being at a large research university, the perspective on Ph.D.'s teaching in my department seems to be that it is a necessary evil. Do it because it helps you to get a job, but don't put too much time into it. In fact, do what you need to do to get a good enough evaluation for the job market, but don't do more.

It is understandable that Ph.D. students' primary training and responsibility is to learn to conduct high-quality research. As such, there are practical limitations to the amount of time and effort that can be devoted to pedagogical training during the Ph.D. program. However, it is lamentable that there seem to be a contingent of students who perceive that teaching quality is actively dismissed in their programs as unimportant. These perceptions imply that research and teaching are mutually exclusive goals. As a discipline with an ethical duty to train future accounting professionals, it is incumbent upon us to fight this perception and to emphasize to future faculty the importance of quality teaching and the complementary relation that exists between teaching and research (Demski & Zimmerman, 2000).

Recommendations

Based on the results of this study, we offer several potential areas of improvement for accounting doctoral programs. First, it could be beneficial for programs to integrate a greater variety of teaching evaluation methods. Our respondents illustrate that many doctoral programs apply an unstructured and unclear teaching evaluation process. This might also explain why the majority of our respondents could not directly identify repercussions of poor teaching performance. Out of several formats of teaching evaluation methods, our respondents indicate that only student evaluations are actively used to evaluate teaching performance. However, several participant comments illustrate that many of the doctoral programs do not provide structured guidance on how to use the student evaluations to improve teaching performance. Therefore, we recommend that doctoral programs provide additional clarity on how to utilize student evaluations to improve teaching and provide additional types of teaching evaluation and more explicit feedback on performance to assure that doctoral students receive adequate and useful teaching feedback.

Based on the benefits highlighted in prior research (e.g., Brightman, 2006) we also encourage the incorporation of mentorships either by faculty members or senior doctoral student cohorts.[12] Across all disciplines, and particularly in accounting, the majority of Ph.D. programs do not have teaching mentoring programs. Interestingly, although very few students reported active teaching mentorships, those who did so rated mentorship as being one of the most helpful training methods. In the open-response comments, several respondents acknowledge that mentorships have helped improve their teaching skills via access to teaching materials, teaching feedback, and general teaching advice. Further, Wygal and Stout (2011) survey accounting faculty who have been formally recognized for their teaching excellence. These teaching exemplars specifically highlight the value of mentorship in improving teaching effectiveness.

Additionally, we suggest that Ph.D. programs consider making the development of a teaching portfolio a requirement. Based on our survey, it appears few programs require doctoral students to develop a teaching portfolio. However, compiling a teaching portfolio is beneficial for several reasons. A portfolio assists in providing an organized means of documenting teaching responsibilities and accomplishments (Babin et al., 2002; Calegari et al., 1999; Stewart, 2004). In addition, the development of the portfolio, in itself, is a useful exercise as similar portfolios are required of faculty for annual reviews and promotion and tenure applications at many universities. Feedback on the portfolio could provide Ph.D. students with valuable information about their teaching accomplishments and their presentation of those accomplishments.[13]

We also recommend that doctoral programs develop effective ways to help prepare non-native English speakers for teaching duties. This preparation will help non-native English speakers enrich their communication, presentation, and classroom management skills. This is of particular importance given that prior research suggests that there is an increasing number of international students in Ph.D. programs, and many of these students pursue faculty positions in the United States (Baldwin, Brown, & Trinkle, 2010; Cho, Roberts, & Roberts, 2008). A study at Purdue University illustrated that other things being equal, students with non-native English speaking instructors (or discussion sections leaders) learned significantly less in each course (Watts & Lynch, 1989). In a follow-up study, Watts and Bosshardt (1992) found that this gap in student learning disappeared when instructors for whom English is a second language were provided with remedial training. Thus, it appears that training beyond the English proficiency standardized tests may be necessary to ensure the adequacy of English skills needed for effective teaching. To this point, several respondents in this study expressed the need for international students to overcome English language difficulties and cultural differences that might appear in their future careers in academia.

Other recommendations include providing structured opportunities for peer discussion, more diverse and complex teaching opportunities, and regular and guided reflection. While we did not specifically address these items in our survey, research on graduate students in various disciplines including humanities, sciences, social sciences, and professional areas (including business) suggests that these are other areas where programs could potentially improve students' preparedness for transitioning into academic careers (Austin, 2002). Finally, consistent with the notion that research and teaching are strong complements to each other (Demski & Zimmerman, 2000), doctoral programs could help Ph.D. students understand ways to integrate their research into their teaching. In doctoral seminars, students could be encouraged to identify appropriate ways to integrate various theories and key research results into the accounting curriculum. Instructors could identify appropriate articles from research journals for use with undergraduate and master's-level accounting students. Incorporating research into teaching might also help the researched-focused doctoral programs (ranked as more prestigious) to place greater emphasis on teaching and better prepare their students for teaching duties without allocating resources away from research.

Limitations and Future Research

This study is subject to several limitations. First, we only survey current Ph.D. students. While current Ph.D. students can provide valuable insight into current pedagogical training practices in doctoral programs, it would also be interesting to survey former Ph.D. students who have transitioned into careers in academia. Former Ph.D. students who are currently in academia would be able to provide a different perspective about the pedagogical preparation their doctoral programs provided. Further, a survey of the junior faculty in the schools highlighted in this study with Ph.D. programs that provide various teaching resources could provide additional insight into the utilization and effectiveness of these resources. Future research could address this. Second, this survey measures *student* perceptions about teaching preparedness and training. A future study could solicit the views of Ph.D. program directors to compare their views to those of Ph.D. students. Finally, as noted previously, this study is descriptive in nature and therefore cannot produce inferences about the effectiveness of teacher preparation programs or a specific discipline's practice with regard to teacher training. In addition, we cannot speak to the value of teaching versus research. Notwithstanding these limitations, this study contributes to the body of literature in accounting education by providing insights into current pedagogical training practices in accounting doctoral programs and by providing comparative data from the related fields of finance, management, and economics.

NOTES

1. A lower proportion of the respondents in accounting were international students compared to the other disciplines.

2. The purpose of the Accounting Education Change Commission (AECC) is to enact changes in accounting education. According to AECC position statement number one, "The need for changes has arisen because accounting programs have not kept pace with the dynamic, complex, expanding, and constantly changing profession for which students are being educated" (AECC, 1990, p. 307). The AAA Pathways Commission was created by the AAA and the AICPA to "study the future structure of higher education for the accounting profession and develop recommendations for educational pathways to engage and retain the strongest possible community of students, academics, practitioners, and other knowledgeable leaders in the practice and study of accounting" (Pathways Commission, 2012, p. 9).

3. We exclude executive and for-profit doctoral programs.

4. From the inception of this study, our goal was to compare various aspects of teaching preparation between accounting doctoral programs and other related doctoral programs (finance, management, and economics). Therefore, we limit our comparison data to programs from universities that have a doctoral program in accounting.

5. We base these statistics on the students listed on program websites. Programs that do not provide contact information for students are not included in these calculations.

6. We thank an anonymous reviewer for noting this important difference.

7. The appropriate internal review board evaluated and approved the study prior to data collection.

8. Results in Tables 4 through 7 reflect unweighted averages reported by discipline. In other words, each school contributes equal weighting to the reported discipline averages. Thus, schools with multiple respondents are weighted equally to schools with one respondent.

9. Course preparations refer to the number of different courses a student teaches in the program. For example, teaching three sections of an Introduction to Accounting class would count as one course preparation.

10. We also examine whether accounting participant responses to these perception questions differ by specialty area (audit, tax, financial, cost, other). Results reveal no significant differences between any groups. In addition, we examine whether accounting participant career aspirations (teaching vs. research vs. service) differ between specialty areas. Results reveal no significant differences between any groups.

11. Note that accounting also had the lowest percentage of international student respondents in our survey. We do not know if this finding obtained in our sample holds in the entire population of doctoral programs. If accounting, as a discipline, has a smaller percentage of international students compared to the other disciplines, then it should come as no surprise that they also have the lowest percentage of programs that require additional proof of English proficiency prior to teaching.

12. See Brightman (2006) for strategies for sustaining a successful teaching mentoring program.

13. See Laverie (2002) and Ouellett (2007) for additional information on the benefits of and strategies for constructing a teaching portfolio.

ACKNOWLEDGMENTS

The authors acknowledge the helpful comments and suggestions made by the editor, two anonymous reviewers, participants from presentations at the 2014 AAA Annual Meeting and Weber State University, Pennie Bagley, Huiqi Gan, Robson Glasscock, Karen Green, David Malone, James Rebele, Melloney Simerly, and Benson Wier.

REFERENCES

AACSB International — The Association to Advance Collegiate Schools of Business (AACSB). (2015). *Eligibility procedures and accreditation standards for business accreditation*. Retrieved from http://www.aacsb.edu/~/media/AACSB/Docs/Accreditation/Standards/2013-bus-standards-update-jan2015.ashx

Accounting Doctoral Scholars (ADS). (2013). *Investing in the future of accounting education*. Retrieved from http://www.adsphd.org/index.asp

Accounting Education Change Commission (AECC). (1990). Objectives of education for accountants: Position statement number one. *Issues in Accounting Education*, 5, 307–312.

Austin, A. E. (2002). Preparing the next generation of faculty: Graduate school as socialization to the academic career. *The Journal of Higher Education, 73*(1), 94–122.

Babin, L. A., Shaffer, T. R., & Tomas, A. M. (2002). Teaching portfolios: Uses and development. *Journal of Marketing Education, 24*(1), 35–42.

Backmon, I. R. (1998). Doctoral accounting candidates: A profile of demographics and perceptions. *Equity & Excellence in Education, 31*(3), 26–36.

Baldwin, A. A., Brown, C. E., & Trinkle, B. S. (2010). Accounting doctoral programs: A multidimensional description. *Advances in Accounting Education: Teaching and Curriculum Innovations, 11*, 101–128.

Behn, B. K., Carnes, G. A., Krull, G. W., Jr., Stocks, K. D., & Reckers, P. M. J. (2008). Accounting doctoral education – 2007 A report to the Joint AAA/APLG/FSA doctoral education committee. *Issues in Accounting Education, 23*(3), 357–367.

Beyer, B., Herrmann, D., Meek, G. K., & Rapley, E. T. (2010). What it means to be an accounting professor: A concise career guide for doctoral students in accounting. *Issues in Accounting Education, 25*(2), 227–244.

Brightman, H. J. (2006). Mentoring faculty to improve teaching and student learning. *Issues in Accounting Education, 21*(2), 127–146.

Brink, A. G., Glasscock, R., & Wier, B. (2012). The current state of accounting Ph.D. programs in the United States. *Issues in Accounting Education, 27*(4), 917–942.

Burton, J. P., Bamberry, N. J., & Harris-Boundy, J. (2005). Developing personal teaching efficacy in new teachers in university settings. *Academy of Management Learning & Education, 4*(2), 160–173.

Calegari, M. J., Geisler, G. G., & Larkins, E. R. (1999). Implementing teaching portfolios and peer reviews in tax courses. *Journal of the American Taxation Association, 21*(2), 95–107.

Chen, J., Liu, Q., & Billger, S. (2013). Where do new Ph.D. economists go? Recent evidence from initial labor market. *Journal of Labor Research, 34*, 312–338.

Chism, N. V. N., & Szabo, B. L. (1997). Teaching awards: The problem of assessing their impact. *To Improve the Academy, 16*, 181–200.

Cho, C. H., Roberts, R. W., & Roberts, S. K. (2008). Chinese students in US accounting and business PhD programs: Educational, political and social considerations. *Critical Perspectives on Accounting, 19*(2), 199–216.

Demski, J. S., & Zimmerman, J. L. (2000). On "research vs. teaching": A long-term perspective. *Accounting Horizons, 14*(3), 343–352.

Eagan, K., Stolzenberg, E. B., Lozano, J. B., Aragon, M. C., Suchard, M. R., & Hurtado, S. (2014). *Undergraduate teaching faculty: The 2013–2014 HERI faculty survey.* Retrieved from http://heri.ucla.edu/monographs/HERI-FAC2014-monograph.pdf

Edwards, J. B., Ingram, R., & Sanders, H. P. (1981). Developing teaching skills in doctoral programs: The current status and perceived needs. *The Accounting Review, 56*, 144–157.

Fogarty, T. J., & Markarian, G. (2007). An empirical assessment of the rise and fall of accounting as an academic discipline. *Issues in Accounting Education, 22*(2), 137–161.

Golde, C. M. (2004). Responsibility of doctoral programs for the career preparation of future faculty. *Peer Review, American Association of Colleges & Universities*, Spring, *6*(3), 26–29.

Gribbin, D. W., Sobery, J., & Braswell, D. (2002). Development of teaching skills in doctoral programs vs. faculty performance evaluation: A survey study. *Advances in Accounting Education: Teaching and Curriculum Innovations, 4*, 87–104.

Hasselback, J. R. (2012). *Hasselback Accounting Directory 2012–2013.* Upper Saddle River, NJ: Pearson Prentice Hall.

Hershey, G. L., Vidyaranya, V. B., & Eatman, J. (1996). Are business doctoral graduates prepared to teach? *Selections, 13*(1), 17–26.

Hopwood, A. G. (2007). Whither accounting research? *The Accounting Review, 82*(5), 1365–1374.

Laverie, D. A. (2002). Improving teaching through improving evaluation: A guide to course portfolios. *Journal of Marketing Education, 24*(2), 104–113.

Ouellett, M. L. (2007). Your teaching portfolio: Strategies for initiating and documenting growth and development. *Journal of Management Education, 31*(3), 421–433.

Pathways Commission. (2012). *The pathways commission: Charting a national strategy for the next generation of accountants.* Retrieved from http://commons.aaahq.org/files/0b14318188/Pathways_Commission_Final_Report_Complete.pdf

Plumlee, R. D., Kachelmeier, S. J., Madeo, S. A., Pratt, J. H., & Krull, G. (2006). Assessing the shortage of accounting faculty. *Issues in Accounting Education, 21*(2), 113–125.

Stammerjohan, W. W., Seifert, D. L., & Guidry, R. P. (2009). Factors affecting initial placement of accounting Ph.Ds. *Advances in Accounting Education: Teaching and Curriculum Innovations, 10*, 103–118.

Stewart, I. (2004). Using portfolios to improve teaching quality: The case of a small business school. *Journal of Education for Business, 80*(2), 75–79.

Stock, W. A., Finegan, T. A., & Siegfried, J. J. (2006). Attrition in economics Ph.D. programs. *American Economic Review, 96*(2), 458–466.

Stock, W. A., Siegfried, J. J., & Finegan, T. A. (2011). Completion rates and time-to-degree in economics PhD programs. *American Economic Review, 101*(3), 176–187.

Utecht, R. L., & Tullous, R. (2009). Are we preparing doctoral students in the art of teaching? *Research in Higher Education Journal, 4*, 1–12. Retrieved from http://www.aabri.com/manuscripts/09195.pdf

Watts, M., & Bosshardt, W. (1992). International teaching assistants and student time allocations: Impacts on learning, grades, and student course and instructor evaluations. Unpublished paper presented at the January meetings of the Allied Social Science Associations.

Watts, M., & Lynch, G. J. (1989). The principles course revisited. *American Economic Review, 79*(2), 236–241.

Wygal, D. E., & Stout, D. E. (2011). The role of continuous improvement and mentoring in the pursuit of teaching effectiveness: Perspectives from award-winning accounting educators. *The Accounting Educators' Journal, 21*(1), 33–44.

NAVIGATING THE ACCOUNTING ACADEMIC JOB MARKET AND RELATED ADVICE

Jason M. Bergner, Joshua J. Filzen and Jeffrey A. Wong

ABSTRACT

Purpose — *To disseminate helpful advice to current and future candidates about the accounting academic job market.*

Methodology/approach — *Literature review, interviews with recently hired faculty members, insights from the author's experiences as both job candidates and search committee members, and discussions with colleagues.*

Findings — *In this chapter, we discuss the current state of the job market for accounting professors and offer our insights as well as those from a group of recent graduates. It is our recent experience that many rookie candidates pursue initial faculty positions with an incomplete understanding of many aspects of the market, including how the market clears, job expectations, and other issues that we believe are important. While others have adequately addressed the importance of research in the profession and alluded to some aspects of the market, we provide additional useful information about the market and other career aspects in order to*

Advances in Accounting Education: Teaching and Curriculum Innovations, Volume 18, 147–176
Copyright © 2016 by Emerald Group Publishing Limited
ISSN: 1085-4622/doi:10.1108/S1085-462220160000018006

assist new graduates in their quests to find fulfilling appointments. Our chapter complements existing literature to form an updated and more complete picture of the market and profession.

Practical implications − *This chapter helps prepare candidates for the job market by providing information and advice that complements advice given in Ph.D. programs and the existing literature.*

Social implications − *Candidates entering the job market will better understand the nuances of the market and can make more informed decisions about the institutions that best meet their needs.*

Originality/value − *The chapter provides important practical advice for job seekers about the accounting academic job market not available elsewhere.*

Keywords: Doctoral education; career advice; job market; academic employment

The vast majority of students in accounting doctoral programs ultimately desire an academic faculty appointment to commence their careers. Existing literature has been effective in addressing the most important aspect of any Ph.D. program − the cultivation of research skills (Beyer, Herrmann, Meek, & Rapley, 2010). There are also papers devoted to entering accounting Ph.D. programs, being successful in Ph.D. programs, and succeeding as a faculty member (Bergner, 2009; Stone, 1996; Hermanson, 2008). However, there is a scarcity of literature addressing the pragmatic aspects of entering the profession. We contribute to the accounting doctoral education literature by providing useful information to help students better understand how the academic job market functions, and information on issues that they should be aware of before entering it. Having a better understanding of the marketplace should enhance the probability of students finding an initial appointment that fits their preferences and gives them the best chance of success. Our chapter is not intended to be a comprehensive career guide, but is designed to complement the existing literature to form a more complete picture of the accounting academic market.

Specifically, this chapter covers information about preparation for the market, including timing issues and its bifurcation. We discuss the various stages of the recruiting and interviewing processes in detail to help job applicants prepare for these eventualities. We also complement existing research by providing a discussion of detailed factors that are important for making an employment decision. These factors are critical to consider in the job selection process and are not formally explained elsewhere. We also provide four supplemental appendices. Appendix A provides a timeline to help candidates identify key dates and milestones in the process. Appendix B provides a listing of common job posting websites. Appendix C contains a sample of detailed questions designed to help the job applicant target their inquiries with prospective employers to help ensure that all valuable information is gathered to make an informed decision. Finally, Appendix D contains a list of the questions we asked recent graduates as part of structured interviews we conducted.

The authors' knowledge base has accrued from recent observations made during extensive job searches and serving on search committees. In addition to our own experiences and collections of informal discussions, we conducted formal structured interviews of individuals with recent job market experience to help form the body of information included in this chapter.[1] Thus, we believe our observations coincide with current market characteristics and make a timely and important contribution to the literature. However, it is important to emphasize that idiosyncrasies of the job market may arise that we do not discuss here. In addition, this chapter is not intended as a criticism of the current state of doctoral advising. In fact, we encourage all doctoral students to gain additional insights and information from trusted advisors.

However, even in programs with adequate job market advising opportunities, much of the information-gathering process is a hodgepodge of conversations with advisors, other Ph.D. students, and outside speakers. Thus, we believe this commentary to be of value even in "well-advised" programs by efficiently disseminating a large volume of relevant information to serve as a foundation for additional information gathering by the student. In fact, when asked whether a consolidated discussion such as this chapter would have been useful, all new faculty members we surveyed responded affirmatively. It should be noted that while our discussion may bring up some points that seem obvious to seasoned professors and market participants, our experiences with new graduates lead us to believe that these same points are not obvious to the majority of them.

While we target this chapter primarily toward new graduates, we also believe this will be of use to recruiting universities that have not recruited candidates recently. Specifically, the section about the job market and recruiting will be of interest to those faculty members who have not participated in the labor market (on either side) for some time. In addition, this chapter can be a resource for advisors of doctoral students by providing assignable reading before beginning an institution-specific discussion. Furthermore, we believe this chapter may have additional value to international students. Students who arrive in the United States for a Ph.D. program are likely unfamiliar with the nuances of the university system and culture in this country. As such, information about the search and hiring process that is often relayed on a more informal level may be of particular use.

In the next section we briefly discuss our chapter in relation to prior literature. Next, we discuss the structured interviews we conducted. We then discuss preparation for the job market in the latter stages of doctoral education, followed by a discussion of job markets and recruiting. After this discussion, we address the detailed factors that should influence candidates' choices, and then briefly discuss candidate communication. A brief conclusion ends the chapter.

PRIOR LITERATURE

Publications providing career advice have largely addressed various aspects of research, including expectations for tenure, maintaining a research stream, publishing guidance, and the review process. Beyer et al. (2010) address these topics in an excellent primer on the subject of career guidance for doctoral students in accounting. The authors properly note the importance of research to the profession, that it is the currency of academics. Beyer et al. (2010) focus on gaining an understanding of the accounting academic environment, as well as research and publishing guidance for new faculty. Our chapter extends this discussion by providing important information about the job market not covered by Beyer et al. (2010) that, in our experience, is being sought by job market entrants.

Additionally, some works in the accounting education literature relate to the job market for accounting academics, but none provide specific discussion of the overall framework of the market and how the market clears. Apostolou, Hassell, Rebele, and Watson (2010) and Apostolou, Dorminey, Hassell, and Watson (2013) conduct a thorough review of the accounting education literature that spans the periods from 2006–2009 and 2010–2012, respectively. Collectively the two papers reviewed 621 articles from the top six journals in which accounting education papers are likely to be published. In support of our assertion that there is a paucity of literature addressing how the job market functions for new Ph.D.s, only 10 papers between Apostolou et al. (2010) and Apostolou et al. (2013) discuss aspects of the job market. Of those papers, the topics covered range from dissertation topics and doctoral student placement statistics to discussing and addressing the shortage of accounting Ph.D.s.

Fogarty, Saftner, and Hasselback (2011) provide information supporting the notion that there is a tier structure that exists in the accounting job market. The prestige of a university where students earn their doctoral degrees is associated with their job placement. The authors find that a majority of doctoral graduates did not place above the prestige (as defined by the tier) of their alma mater, suggesting a ceiling effect for graduates. Baldwin, Brown, and Trinkle (2010) also study doctoral programs and placement but examine a wider range of variables, including endowed faculty positions and administrative roles. Our chapter complements these papers by providing a broad description of the labor market process, its participants (hiring schools), and the timing and clearing of the market.

Hunt, Eaton, and Reinstein (2009) examine factors that drive job acceptance decisions for new and relocating accounting faculty. The authors base the study on surveys that include 37 factors of importance, including salary, teaching loads, and the existence of a Ph.D. program. Findings for new faculty indicate that teaching loads, compatibility with other faculty, and support available for research are among the most important factors for job selection. Our chapter extends this work by providing insights not revealed by Hunt et al. (2009), including a more detailed discussion of why some of the most important factors related to job acceptance matter and how the job search process itself is structured.

STRUCTURED INTERVIEWS

To provide additional perspective for the chapter, we conducted nine structured telephone interviews from a self-generated participant list after obtaining approval from the appropriate university Institutional Review Board (IRB) office. We include our question list in Appendix D. In generating the participant list, we focused on recently hired accounting professors (Ph.D. graduation date of 2013 or later), with no more than any two participants graduating from or currently employed at the same institution. We offered the participants a confidential setting to encourage candid responses. We have both formally and informally integrated information from these interviews throughout the chapter. With each included response, we note whether the response came from a participant at a research university, balanced university, or teaching university.

Despite our relatively small sample size of participants, we sought a wide cross section of recent Ph.D. graduates. Five interviewees are currently employed at universities with a doctoral program in accounting (which we call research universities), three are at balanced schools, and one is at a school primarily focused on teaching. Three participants classified themselves as international students when in the doctoral program, six conduct primarily archival research, and six are male.

When entering the market initially, the participants' strategies for securing a job varied with respect to the fall and spring markets. Three interviewees targeted the fall market specifically, citing desires to find a position at a more "balanced" school and wanting to get a job as soon as possible. However, two others went to the fall market to search out any research (Ph.D. granting) schools that might be interviewing, with plans to continue into the spring market. Both ended up taking fall offers from research schools. Three other interviewees specifically targeted the spring market, including Rookie Camp. Interestingly, only one of these three ended up accepting an offer from a research school. One other interviewee admitted to having no particular strategy in a fall versus spring context.

With regard to potential employers' expectations about works-in-progress, participants' perceptions varied widely, even within school types. While all schools were interested in the dissertation, some teaching and balanced schools did not inquire much about other works, but instead focused on the timeline for completing the dissertation. We believe it is fair to say that both the quality and number of working papers in the pipeline were important to almost all schools, with quality being most important to provide an assessment of potential, especially at more research-focused schools. In addition to a high-quality dissertation, participants suggested research schools desired at least one other high-quality co-authored paper with high potential for publication, perhaps under review at a top journal. Participants suggested that candidates with an R&R (revise and resubmit) at a top journal possessed an extremely valuable signal.

The advice these candidates received when on the market varied widely. Four of the participants emphasized advice of a personal nature, such as finding the right "fit," being happy, and geography issues. Four emphasized the advice on research, while one admitted to "not getting much advice at all."

Of particular interest to readers may be participants' responses to the question about common mistakes job candidates make (Appendix D, question 13). Four interviewees focused on mistakes that could be classified as "soft skills." Included here were trying too hard to impress the interviewer, not being prepared for the interview, not doing enough/any research on the school itself, and not appreciating fit. One participant noted, in reference to international students, the importance of being proficient with English.

Other participants focused on mistakes from a research perspective. These observed errors include trying to edit the road paper at the last minute, coming onto the market before the candidate's research was "ready," presentation quality during the interview, and confidence in one's research.

Finally, all participants agreed that they would have found a paper on job market specifics very valuable during their time as students, and they also supported a sample question set that could be used as a resource during interviews. We elaborate on these (and other) topics throughout the remainder of the chapter.

PREPARATION FOR ENTERING THE JOB MARKET

Typically, students will have preliminary interviews with universities, sometimes up to a year before the job start date. Therefore, would-be candidates must begin to prepare for the job search well in advance. We have included a timeline in Appendix A as a reference for this discussion. The first step in preparing for the job market is to consider what type of school a candidate would like to work at, as this may affect the timeline necessary for completing the dissertation.

The most important priority for entering the market is to ensure the dissertation is on track to be completed before the anticipated employment start date. Ideally, students will have defended their proposal and will be making significant strides to complete their dissertation the summer prior to the academic year in which they plan to graduate. Students should work with their committee, particularly the chair, to develop a realistic timeline that can be followed for the proposal defense, dissertation defense, and completion of Ph.D. requirements. Communication and coordination with the dissertation committee is crucial during the doctoral program, especially leading into the final year of study. Depending on the student's committee, the student may need to take a more assertive role in getting timeline estimates. While students may run the risk of bothering committee members, at this point students must understand that it is their responsibility to finish the dissertation process.

The student's options for employment will be limited if there is not a reasonably definitive dissertation timeline to communicate to prospective employers. Not being able to provide reasonable certainty to prospective employers sends a negative signal about the candidate's ability to finish by the job start date, which may lead to a decision not to extend a campus interview/offer to an otherwise attractive candidate. Thus, ensuring that the committee is committed to a reasonably firm timeline is essential.

A student without a clear timeline to graduation may be limited to recruiting with employers willing to hire ABD candidates ("All But Dissertation," which commonly refers to a candidate who has completed all of the graduation requirements, except for the dissertation), as many universities will require the completion of the Ph.D. before officially hiring. While some students may initially consider an ABD offer, there are at least two reasons why it is in the candidate's best interest to finish the dissertation before embarking upon a new job.

First, even for those universities that are willing to allow a new hire to begin working ABD, there may be a significant salary reduction in combination with a higher teaching load. For instance, the contract may state that the new hire will be paid at a salary less than a tenure-track faculty member (e.g., the salary for a full-time instructor) until the dissertation is finished, and may have the corresponding teaching load of an instructor. Moreover, the contract may also state that the new hire's dissertation must be finished by the end of the first year to continue employment. Second, a new hire's tenure clock may have started while the new hire is trying to finish the dissertation.

It is a significant burden to carry an unfinished dissertation into a new faculty position. Coordination and communication issues with dissertation committee members often become more difficult when students leave their home university, and unanticipated complications may arise that delay the completion of their degree. Of course, it follows that any unexpected complications will only exacerbate the already less than desirable situation. The new hire may be: (a) under pressure to finish the dissertation, while (b) likely teaching new classes that require extensive preparation, (c) acclimating to a new culture, both at the university and community levels, and (d) trying to start other research projects in order to meet tenure requirements.

However, the previous discussion about not being able to finish the dissertation and leaving ABD should not be confused with a strategic decision to go ABD to obtain a longer tenure clock. With full support of your committee, a strategic plan to leave ABD with minimal penalties can be an advantageous arrangement with proper planning and support. Generally, this is an arrangement that is more common among research-oriented universities.

Another priority for entering the market should be having other scholarly works in addition to the dissertation. The dissertation may commence a stream of work that can carry an entire career. However, solely relying upon the dissertation for all scholarly work can be a risky strategy. At every opportunity possible, students should generate ideas that turn into projects and can be moved into the publication pipeline (see Beyer et al., 2010; Stone, 1996 for further discussion). First- and second-year papers, if assigned, provide such opportunities. These opportunities not only provide potential publications, but also provide an opportunity to start working with co-authors, who may be current professors at the student's university, other Ph.D. students in the department, or other students and/or professors met at conferences, workshops, and seminars (see Nathan, Hermanson, & Hermanson, 1998 for more details about co-authoring). Based on our experience and collection of additional interview data, the exact number and stages of projects expected of candidates is highly variable, even among similar school types. Every university will be extremely interested in the dissertation and progression toward graduation. Beyond that, candidates will need to demonstrate they have the potential to publish in journals sufficient to be successful at the target university.

Having research projects in addition to the dissertation can differentiate a student from others in the market and help to land the job he/she wants. Having multiple papers (both solo and co-authored) sends a signal that the applicant has the potential to generate multiple high-quality ideas and work both alone and with others successfully. Works-in-progress will also help reduce the stress associated with the transition to a new job. Students should not underestimate the time and effort needed to acclimate to a new culture, both within the university, college, and department, but also the surrounding community and area of the country, which also may be new. During this transition it may be more difficult to be productive from a research standpoint.

JOB MARKET AND RECRUITING

Understanding how the accounting job market functions is critical to some of the planning discussed in the prior section. Preparation during the doctoral program will help the student confidently engage in the process of applying for jobs, having preliminary interviews, and going on-campus visits. We begin by first discussing the different types of universities recruiting and how to identify a university's focus, followed by a discussion of the job market with observations on timing, from inception to clearing.

From a research perspective, schools generally fall into those with faculty duties that are teaching-dominant, research-dominant, or those with a balanced proportion of the two. The presence of an accounting Ph.D. program is a quick metric to classify a program as research-dominant, but research focus can still be variable across universities regardless of the presence of a Ph.D. program. Most department websites provide enough information for candidates to get a sense of the publication records of current faculty, which is generally a better metric of research expectations/focus. Asking the recruiting committee chair about research expectations in an initial interaction is also a great way to uncover useful information about the department's focus. From a non-research perspective, other factors such as teaching interests, climate, family location, and culture may further narrow students' focus. Understanding the kind of school that one wants to work for will help to focus on appropriate schools.

Timing of the Market

The market for new faculty is generally bifurcated. Usually teaching and balanced schools will conduct campus interviews in the fall (discussed first), which generally includes schools that do not have Ph.D. programs. Schools with Ph.D. programs typically interview in the spring. Schools that interview in the fall typically aim for obtaining accepted offers by the end of the calendar year. Screening for fall interviews usually begins during the preceding summer, often at the annual American Accounting Association (AAA) meeting held in August. Screening interviews have become so commonplace at the annual AAA meeting that special interview facilities have been made available for interviewing universities to rent.

Additionally, the online AAA Career Center is a convenient source of job postings for all types of universities. There is normally significant job posting activity in preparation for the AAA annual meeting (during June and July). See Appendix B for a listing of common job posting websites, most of which offer email subscriptions for notifications of new job postings. Keeping close tabs on these and other related sites can help candidates identify which schools plan to interview at the AAA meeting. This in turn allows candidates more time to screen the schools in an effort to find a likely match.

Students may benefit by taking a proactive approach, contacting schools directly (the Search Committee Chair normally is listed as the contact in the job posting) to ascertain whether the school may be a potential match. Taking such steps not only sends a positive signal to the potential employer, but it also allows candidates to have an initial personal contact with someone at the university. This personal contact may reveal information about the school not contained in a job posting (which may have more of a boilerplate feel) and thus give candidates additional information in determining whether the school might be a potential fit.

A common practice for a university in the fall market, as mentioned earlier, is to conduct screening interviews of candidates at the AAA meeting. The interviews usually take place with a small number (2–3) of the accounting faculty from the university. The faculty holding interviews are likely to be among the more successful and research active people from that school. These individuals are a good gauge of the caliber of faculty that the school wants, and can lend important insights into the culture of the faculty.

These 2–3 faculty members may interview up to 15 people or more each day, and the interviews may last for three days in total. Thus, candidates should aspire to make a lasting impression with faculty from schools in which they have interest. The purpose of the AAA interviews is to screen the candidates into a smaller pool for the next step in the interview process, which is usually a phone interview. Prior to both the screening and phone interviews, it is important for job seekers to have a list of questions to ask, since the quality of an applicant's questions is often evaluated by the interviewers. Anecdotally, all of our participants expressed their support for having a set of questions as a reference tool for interviews.

Interviewee (Balanced University): I wish I had known what questions to ask that would help me assess my fit with the interviewing university.

Interviewee (Research University): There are awkward silences in offices. Having a list to fall back on would be handy.

The phone (or video) interviews may be conducted with a larger portion of the faculty; generally, any interested faculty member may choose to sit in on these phone interviews. The purpose of the phone interviews is to narrow candidates down into a smaller list for potential campus visits. From here, schools may choose to bring candidates to campus in a number of ways. For example, some schools may bring in three candidates on three different days and then decide to whom (if anyone) they wish to make an offer. Other schools may bring their candidates in one at a time and make a decision on that candidate before moving on (if necessary) to the next.

At virtually every school's campus visit, candidates will make a research presentation. Candidates may also be asked to do a teaching demonstration at schools that emphasize teaching ability to a greater degree. During these presentations, multiple skills will be assessed, including the ability to communicate, think on one's feet, answer questions, teach, and whether a person would be a good colleague. The information gathering is bilateral. During the presentation, job candidates may assess the collegiality of the faculty present along with their research skills and intellect. The latter two qualities are important because it is desirable to be among scholars if one wishes to produce quality scholarship.

The campus interview will also typically include opportunities to meet with both faculty members and administrators such as the Dean and members of the Provost's office. The discussions with an administrator will typically involve less detail about the day-to-day duties of a faculty member and more about the department and college.

Because candidates' understanding of how well they fit with a potential employer is so important, we have included a sample set of questions for candidates to consider in Appendix C. This question set should be useful throughout all stages of the interview process.

Schools with Ph.D. programs often conduct on-campus interviews in the spring. Thus, universities trying to recruit in the spring may or may not formally interview candidates at the annual AAA meeting, although faculty from Ph.D.-granting institutions often attend the AAA meeting in August and may pursue informal interviews.

For research schools, the expectation is that the candidate will present a polished draft of their dissertation during an on-campus interview, which constrains this market in terms of timing. This is at least one reason for the bifurcation of the market, as many schools recruiting in the fall will find presentation of co-authored work or earlier stage drafts of the dissertation to be acceptable. In either case, the objective for most universities interviewing during a particular academic year is to hire faculty to start the following fall.

In recent years, the hiring process for Ph.D.-granting institutions has accelerated to coincide with the "Rookie Camp," a two-day event hosted by the University of Miami (rookiecamp.org), where candidates briefly present their research and interview with interested universities.

Our conversations and interactions with colleagues revealed that many initially viewed the camp to be a more research-oriented market. This was likely due to its timing. The camp is hosted during the first week of December and begins at a time when many teaching-heavy and balanced universities are hoping to have their search process finished (i.e., they interview starting at the AAA annual meeting and begin bringing candidates to campus in October). Thus, because many universities that fall into these latter two groups would be likely finishing their searches, the Rookie Camp was initially associated with the more research-dominant schools that recruit more heavily in the spring market.

However, we note that of the 89 participating institutions sending Ph.D. candidates and the 85 universities participating with job postings in December 2013 (the fourth year of the Camp), there appears to be a mix of Ph.D.-granting institutions of all tiers (55 schools), non-Accounting Ph.D.-granting schools (29 schools), and even non-academic participants (1 institution). Thus, the perception that the Rookie Camp is heavily research focused appears to be an oversimplification of its function.

The Rookie Camp may eventually result in a closer alignment of the accounting faculty job market with other disciplines within the business school, which often have their annual meetings and initial screening interviews closer to the end of the calendar year. On the other hand, the presence of a greater number of non-research schools may be explained by the non-research schools not finding a suitable candidate in the fall and deciding to try again at the camp.

Anecdotally, participants who targeted the spring market and went to Rookie Camp commented about the participating schools being of a wider range than expected. Further, as new professors, at least one participant (now at a research school) noted that the current Ph.D. students have commented on the range of schools being even wider.

Informal conversations with the camp representatives from participating research schools reveal a belief that many students simply do not know in August if they will be ready to graduate by the end of the current academic year. Thus, schools at the Rookie Camp may have greater confidence that the later start date will yield candidates with a clearer picture of their paths to graduation.

The 2013 Rookie Camp marked the first year the camp was co-sponsored with the AAA, with the AAA providing organizational support. Our discussion with the AAA reveals that both recruiting events (the AAA annual meeting and the Rookie Camp) are planned to continue indefinitely. However, we speculate that in time there could be a shift away from recruiting at the AAA annual meeting (at least for new graduates) if a candidate could essentially recruit with a variety of school types at the Rookie

Camp. If that were to happen, the AAA meeting may become more of a venue for schools with a heavy teaching focus, as well as a place for faculty looking to relocate to begin their search. Given the trend toward the Rookie Camp becoming an important recruiting event for all types of schools, our advice to all candidates is that they should be prepared to attend the Rookie Camp. Recruiting delays or lack of offers from target schools in the fall may necessitate attendance at the Rookie Camp.

Broad Factors to Consider When Targeting Universities

Strategically, students would be wise to apply for jobs at a number of schools since screening and hiring decisions are often less than predictable. The accounting academic job market is often thought to be a multi-period game. One major contributing factor for this multi-period description is the unpredictability of the market a job candidate enters (Hunt et al., 2009). We believe most job candidates are risk averse, and when combined with expiring job offers being presented in a non-ideal order, the effect can be a less than optimal initial placement resulting in costly relocation in the future. Candidates and recruiters may be wise to consider this in their recruitment efforts.

Universities interview multiple candidates, and candidates typically interview at multiple universities. Just as universities screen for their finalists, job seekers should carefully screen schools for potential matches. Although it would be relatively easy to apply to a large number of universities, students should understand that their time is valuable, especially during the final year when they are trying to finish a dissertation, develop working papers, and keep up with the normal duties of being a Ph.D. student. Traveling, presenting, and interviewing are exhausting activities. Thus, failing to properly screen for potential matches can result in spending time inefficiently.

Candidates should also consider reputational costs associated with accepting interviews without serious consideration of accepting a job offer with the university. Accounting faculty expend a great deal of time and effort interviewing candidates. Learning later that the candidate may not have had a genuine interest in the school could have repercussions.

There are a number of factors that must be weighed by the student when choosing an institution at which to seek employment. The most important initial decision doctoral students need to make is which of the three types of schools they wish to work at: research-dominant, balanced, or teaching-dominant. Not all universities fall neatly into one of the three categories, but the general classification is useful to screen school types.

Research-dominant universities generally would be those with active Ph.D. programs. Advantages of working at a research-dominant university generally include a higher base salary and more resources for conducting research and fewer teaching responsibilities. Participants in our study who are currently employed at research schools confirmed the depth of their resources.

Interviewee (Research University): There are no research budget limitations per se, but unusual requests do need special approval.

The comment above from a participant at a research-dominant university highlights the research focus and willingness of those departments to support research financially. Some examples of specific resources available at research-dominant universities (that are likely to be more limited elsewhere) include expensive data subscriptions, funds to pay research study participants, access to experimental labs, access to advanced research assistants (i.e., Ph.D. students), regular research workshops, and ability to travel to multiple conferences per year. The cost of these benefits is higher research expectations, which can lead to more pressure and less certainty about tenure. Some departments may expect mentoring of Ph.D. students before earning tenure as well.

Of these research-dominant universities, there is a prestige structure described by Fogarty et al. (2011), who provide evidence of a ceiling effect in Ph.D. programs. That is, most graduates of Ph.D. programs will not obtain a faculty position at a school in a higher tier than they attend as a student. Students are often advised to obtain employment with the best research school possible. This corresponds to a maxim often spoken to students that it is easier to move down than up.

Balanced schools value and reward both research and teaching activity. Generally, the need to produce "A" level publications (top 3–6 journals) at balanced schools is far less than with research-dominant schools. Evidence from Walker, Fleischman, and Stephenson (2010) suggest that the top six journals are generally considered to be (in no particular order) *The Accounting Review*; *Journal of Accounting and Economics*; *Journal of Accounting Research*; *Contemporary Accounting Research*; *Accounting, Organizations, & Society*; and *Review of Accounting Studies*. Teaching quality is more heavily weighted at balanced schools, but usually is insufficient by itself to warrant promotion and tenure.

Teaching-dominant schools will emphasize teaching quality but will also value scholarship, especially those schools that are AACSB (Association to Advance Collegiate Schools of Business) accredited, since maintaining accreditation requires a minimum amount of scholarship. Graduates entering the job market will generally be well received by balanced and teaching-dominant schools if they do well in the classroom and engage in productive scholarship.

Strategically, students should consider that if they focus solely on the research schools that tend to hire in the spring market and do not secure employment, they would likely miss employment opportunities with the other types of schools. On the other hand, balanced and teaching schools will often want a candidate to accept an offer prior to the spring market. Thus, candidates will find it difficult to obtain an offer from a fall market school and then wait to see if a spring market school offers as well. While some candidates might initially find this to be an attractive strategy, the long-term repercussions of reneging on a signed offer in a small community such as accounting would exceed any perceived benefit. Therefore, candidates should carefully consider which market they want to participate in and screen schools accordingly.

DETAILED FACTORS WHEN MAKING AN EMPLOYMENT DECISION

Understanding the factors that will make one successful helps a candidate to select the right set of universities with which to interview and subsequently, the right university from which to accept a job. The base salary is a central financial figure since other benefits are often linked to it such as pension contributions, merit raises, cost of living increases, and summer support. Other factors that new faculty are most concerned with are teaching load, criteria for getting tenure, compatibility with other faculty, and geography (Hunt et al., 2009). Before discussing these and other factors in detail, we provide a brief overview of the duties that most faculty perform.

Faculty have three major components of their job: research, teaching, and service. Schools should provide candidates with some idea of the relative breakdown of their duties. For example, a school may break down research/teaching/service percentages as 50/40/10. The weighting of these three elements will give the job candidate a fairly clear picture of what is expected of them during the first years of their employment. However, we note that the percentages used for weighting evaluations most likely will not equal the percentage of time a faculty member spends in each area.

At most schools, of the three job components, research and teaching performance (in that order) are the most important dimensions to achieve promotion to associate professor and obtain tenure. Further, research performance has by far the most external capital and will lead to more options should the faculty member choose (or need) to re-enter the market at a future point. Teaching quality may have more or less external capital, depending on the school. Knowing the general expectations of a school along the three dimensions of research, teaching, and service will allow the candidate to more effectively screen for potential matches.

Research Resources

Research resources of potential employers are important for at least two reasons. First, there must be a match between the research expectations for tenure and the resources provided. For instance, schools requiring "A" publications should provide resources consistent with those needed to obtain such publications. Candidates should be wary of schools with high research expectations and a low level of resources to support research. Candidates should also be wary of schools with high research expectations if the candidate's particular research interests and methods do not fit within the scope of the university's target journal list (either explicitly or implicitly).

Second, greater research resources enable greater productivity, which increases marketability in the long term. Thus, candidates should carefully consider whether the school has the types of data needed to support their research. Additionally, resources should not be construed to only mean access to databases or participants for experimental studies. Research support for attending conferences, summer compensation, course releases, networking with colleagues, purchasing new software, books, and other items are also important factors to consider.

Other research factors include faculty interaction, mentoring, and time. Note whether the faculty have a history and current practice of co-authoring papers with one another. Department websites and literature searches can help with this task. Co-authoring papers suggests a collegial environment and increased possibilities for fitting into a research-oriented group. When faculty are willing to co-author with new hires, it indicates that they will have a vested interest in the success of the new faculty.

Faculty with research interests consistent with the job candidate are likely to be a valuable resource. However, there is no guarantee that they will be good mentors or will stay at the hiring institution. It is therefore a good idea to get a sense of the department's culture. Ask whether the department is committed to some form of mentorship for new faculty and what that might specifically entail. Ideally, there would be more than one mentor for a new faculty member to work with and the department would have a culture of mentorship. Additionally, consider that faculty in the other departments on campus may have comparable research interests and may prove to be a valuable resource for conducting research.

Teaching and Service Duties

Faculty candidates should also carefully consider teaching expectations, since more time spent on teaching necessarily means less time for research. Most students who have taught will recognize the importance of and distinction between the number of distinct courses taught per year (preps) versus the number of sections taught per year (load). The number of preps taught can greatly influence the amount of time spent devoted to teaching.

Universities with Masters programs will have a larger number of classes to cover and this may affect the average number of preps per faculty member (scheduling and department size also play a role). For some, this may be a concern, but for others this may be an opportunity to teach advanced courses that align with teaching or research interests. Class size also matters. Smaller numbers of students are generally more manageable, especially for upper-division courses that require the delivery and assessment of more technical material.

Also important are the number of contact hours. For instance, teaching a three-unit course requires fewer contact hours than teaching a course that is four units. Teaching days matter as well. Some schools feature courses that are taught three days per week (MWF) and others two days per week (MW). If it is possible to block teaching days into two days per week, larger blocks of uninterrupted time can be devoted to research. Find out whether graduate or student assistants are available to help with teaching (or research) duties. Having a few hours of help per week will free up time that can be used to pursue scholarship.

Teaching assignments can be highly variable between universities. Accordingly, this affects time available for research. Be wary of schools with high research expectations in conjunction with time-consuming teaching assignments.

Candidates can and should leverage their teaching experience in the Ph.D. program when applying for jobs. Most hiring universities will have an ideal set of courses they would like covered by a new hire. Interest in teaching the course(s) that need to be covered will be necessary in most cases, and experience teaching the course(s) will be highly desirable. While we generally do not recommend taking on additional preps in the Ph.D. program unnecessarily, some programs may allow Ph.D. students to teach courses they would like to teach in the future. Generally, teaching courses other than introductory courses will make a candidate much more marketable, especially with less research-focused schools. Teaching the same course(s) taught in the Ph.D. program at the hiring institution will greatly reduce the amount of time needed to devote toward teaching as well.

Faculty provide service to govern departments, colleges, and the university. Service will be an integral part of the job. Generally, service will constitute the smallest percentage of an assistant professor's role, increasing with promotion to associate professor. There is usually an inverse relationship between the amount of time expected to be spent on research versus service activities. As service has nearly zero external capital, candidates should be wary of schools that require a great deal of service from non-tenured professors.

Tenure-Related Factors

Tenure and promotion is the first major milestone in the careers of most accounting academics. Some schools will offer a fairly concrete idea of the requirements for tenure, although it is not uncommon to be provided a vague notion of what constitutes a tenurable record. In cases where the tenure requirements are vague, ask to see the Curriculum Vitae of the last tenured faculty member. Similarly, ask about the record of the last professor denied tenure and any specific factors that led to the denial. Schools with a history of not granting tenure to assistant professors may be riskier for candidates looking to permanently locate.

Keep in mind that standards can change (usually upward). Often, this is because of changes in administration (Deans and/or College Presidents). While it is understandable to be somewhat preoccupied with obtaining tenure, the goal after 5 years of employment should be to have the choice about whether to remain and apply for tenure and promotion, or whether to leave and find a job elsewhere. Although it may seem somewhat counter-intuitive at first, having a focus on remaining marketable can increase the chance of obtaining tenure.

Universities vary with respect to formal review schedules. While some universities conduct annual evaluations, others may conduct biannual evaluations. Another source of variation is the level of the review, which may be major in some years and minor in other years. Candidates should ask about the evaluation schedule to ensure that the environment suits their needs for feedback.

Geographical Factors

Of all the factors not directly related to the job, geographical preference is probably the most important. Hunt et al. (2009) find that faculty going to teaching/balanced schools emphasized geography over salary in their search criteria. Candidates should thoroughly research the locales of schools that invite them in for campus visits. The size of the area (population), culture, proximity to desirable locations, and other factors can not only be important to the candidate but the candidate's family as well. Much can be found about the cost of real estate, relative cost of living, safety, and cultural activities. As mentioned earlier, we have included in Appendix B a sample listing of questions for candidates to help screen potential employers. This list also includes some questions to help with these additional aspects of job selection criteria.

Culture and Fit

Fit is a difficult concept to describe, as it encompasses a combination of all the previously discussed factors and more. In addition to what we have already discussed, candidates need to find a place where they will be comfortable and can participate in a collegial environment. Fit often includes intangibles that involve the personalities of the candidate, potential colleagues, campus environment, and other factors.

Candidates should ask questions to assess whether their work styles and personality would be a good match. These could be factors such as how working from home is perceived, if faculty socialize outside of business hours, whether faculty make a point to celebrate each other's accomplishments, how much input faculty have in the timing of their teaching schedules, whether there is a supportive environment for women and minorities, etc. Because this concept has a certain amount of opacity, specific questions will have high variability between both candidates and schools.

The best advice we can give is to ask questions related to the elements of fit candidates find important and to follow their instincts. Our experiences lead us to believe that although fit is difficult to quantify, it is often detectible during campus visits. Our structured interviews also bear out the importance of this variable, as finding a good fit was a commonly and voluntarily offered theme.

> Interviewee (Research University): A common mistake candidates make is not appreciating fit as much as they should. They might focus more on rankings or other criteria.

> Interviewee (Balanced University): The best piece of advice I received was "find the right fit."

A hostile work environment is not normally a productive environment. We recommend Hermanson (2008) for additional discussion about institutional and departmental culture for additional advice in this area. Another good source would be to seek out observations from faculty who have worked at multiple schools. Their experiences can reveal insights into the benefits (costs) of a good (poor) fit.

Negotiation

Assuming an offer is made, many candidates seek advice for agreeing upon the terms with their new employer. First, generally, it is *not* offensive to ask for amendments or additions to the written offer, so long as the requests are specific, reasonable, and justifiable. For example, the candidate may have other campus visits scheduled and may need another week or two to consider the offer. Honesty is the best approach in such a situation.

If the candidate would like to complete scheduled visits, the candidate should try to extend the decision making time period. While the offering school understands candidates are interviewing at multiple schools and will have some flexibility accordingly, the candidate must understand that the school does not have unlimited flexibility. If the candidate would like to accept the offer and not complete the remaining visits, the candidate should call the remaining schools before accepting the offer to see how they would like to proceed. This specific situation can be difficult to navigate, and ultimately we recommend candidates consult with a trusted advisor if they find themselves in such a precarious situation.

Other than the timeline of the offer, negotiated items generally fall into three categories: compensation, teaching arrangements, and research resources. These topics have been previously discussed but should be considered negotiable until proven otherwise. The time for negotiation is after an offer has been extended, but before acceptance. It is important for job candidates to consider that the terms of employment may stay fairly static after being hired, so any aspects of the job that are suboptimal should be discussed before accepting an offer. Negotiating any terms of an offer require diplomacy and tact on the part of the candidate. While obtaining the best package possible is important, this must be balanced with the appearance of seeming pushy and/or difficult. Our discussion is not a treatise on contract negotiation but is intended to highlight the variables that may be negotiated.

The base salary dominates any other element of the compensation package. The degree to which it can be negotiated depends on many factors such as budgetary constraints, union contracts, and whether the maximum amount authorized was used to craft the offer. Although the key component of compensation is the base salary, summer support is a material form of compensation. Summer support is supplemental to the base salary, and compensates faculty members in order to continue their research projects during the summer months. The amount and duration of summer support may be negotiable.

Depending upon the type of university, teaching duties are likely to consume a large proportion of the candidate's time. The effort spent teaching will depend largely upon the amount of preparation required for a course, number of students enrolled in the course, and number of preparations for courses per year. It is important to arrive at a teaching schedule that is mutually beneficial for both the job candidate and university. The availability of teaching assistance from graduate or other students can greatly assist in managing the time spent on teaching.

Examples of research resources include purchasing databases, software, or hardware necessary for research. Research assistance may be available in the form of a graduate student assistant. While not necessarily discussed in the offer, consider looking at the university's available electronic journals, statistical software, and other resources to see if any needed resources are not currently available.

Keep in mind that accommodations requested may come at a cost to the other faculty (e.g., a course release). A wise candidate should have all of the important accommodations written into the employment contract. It is usually easier to ask for something during negotiation than upon arrival, especially if what is being asked for is outside of normal procedure.

If candidates have not already discussed available help for finding a spouse employment, information on local schools, or other family resources, this would be a good time to ask. In general, a candidate will have a greater probability of getting prompt information during the negotiation process.

CANDIDATE COMMUNICATION

Communication throughout the recruiting process is critical. As we suggested previously, contacting the search committee at the beginning of the search process to gain additional insights before a formal application is submitted is wise on the candidate's part to save both sides substantial time if it becomes clear that the position is not a good match to the candidate.

Interviewee (Research University): Some schools send mixed messages in their job postings. For instance, schools might specify a specific need, and sometimes that is for a teaching need, sometimes for a research need, or perhaps even both.

It is important to find out from the committee chair exactly who the ideal candidate is for the university and what factors the university considers ideal but not required. Similarly, the candidate should ask at each stage of the interview process what the timeline is for the search committee in regards to the next step of the process (phone interview, campus visit, extending an offer).

The candidate should always proactively update the committee about their status. Other good reasons to contact the committee would be to follow up with specific questions or send a thank you note. Although it is wise not to badger the committee, once the period of time the committee laid out for making a decision has passed, the candidate should be proactive about following up with the committee. Unfortunately, sometimes notifying candidates that they did not make it to the next stage of the process is not high on the search committee's priority list. Thus, the candidate should plan to follow up at reasonable intervals.

In addition, the candidate should follow general advice on interviewing etiquette. This includes sending notes of thanks (either electronically or by mail), being respectful, and maintaining a professional appearance. There are many resources for general interview etiquette available for a candidate needing this type of advice (e.g., Chaney & Martin, 2007). One issue that does catch some candidates off guard is that alcohol consumption at dinners or social gatherings is common in the recruiting process. The best advice we can offer candidates is to drink only if others have ordered first and to always avoid intoxication.

CONCLUSION

Our chapter provides students of doctoral programs with knowledge about the job market that complements their development of research skills in the doctoral program. Recent experiences by the authors in searches to recruit faculty revealed that many job candidates were inadequately informed about many aspects of the job market, recruiting, and other factors to consider when choosing an academic position. We wrote our chapter to help fill this void in candidates' knowledge.

A better understanding of how the job market and recruiting process functions should allow candidates to properly prepare themselves for the job search and determine the goodness of fit for a particular job opportunity. While some aspects of the job market and nature of recruiting may undergo change in the coming years, the nature of accounting faculty positions is likely to remain similar. We believe our discussion about preliminary and campus interviews, and the factors important to making employment decisions will remain relevant for some time.

There are at least two opportunities for future research in this area. First, there are many idiosyncrasies that occur in a job search, and as such we were unable to cover every scenario within the scope of this chapter. Future research could explore the creation of a troubleshooting guide to help candidates through other difficult circumstances that may present themselves in the interviewing process. Second, we have primarily taken a student focus in this chapter. Although our discussions are applicable to recruiters interested in the market as well, future work could explore recruiting-specific issues as well.

NOTE

1. We thank two anonymous referees with recent job market experience for providing their experiences as well.

ACKNOWLEDGMENTS

We thank Jannet Vreeland, Brian Williams, and Shan Wang for their helpful comments and suggestions. Special thanks to Kurt Gardner at the American Accounting Association for helpful discussion, and Andrew Jenkins for his research assistance.

REFERENCES

Apostolou, B., Dorminey, J. W., Hassell, J. M., & Watson, S. F. (2013). Accounting education literature review (2010–2012). *Journal of Accounting Education, 31*(2), 107–161.

Apostolou, B., Hassell, J. M., Rebele, J. E., & Watson, S. F. (2010). Accounting education literature review (2006–2009). *Journal of Accounting Education, 28*(3–4), 145–197.

Baldwin, A. A., Brown, C. E., & Trinkle, B. S. (2010). Accounting doctoral programs: A multidimensional perspective. *Advances in Accounting Education: Teaching and Curriculum Innovations, 11*, 101–128.

Bergner, J. (2009). Pursuing a Ph.D. in accounting: Walking in with your eyes open. *Journal of Accountancy, 207*(3), Web exclusive article. Retrieved from http://www.journalofaccountancy.com/Web/PursuingaPhDinAccounting

Beyer, B., Herrmann, D., Meek, G. K., & Rapley, E. T. (2010). What it means to be an accounting professor: A concise career guide for doctoral students in accounting. *Issues in Accounting Education, 25*(2), 227–244.

Chaney, L. H., & Martin, J. S. (2007). *The essential guide to business etiquette.* Westport, CT: Greenwood Publishing Group.

Fogarty, T. J., Saftner, D. V., & Hasselback, J. R. (2011). Knowing one's place: The distribution of new accounting academics into a segmented labor market. *Journal of Accounting Education, 29*(2–3), 89–99.

Hermanson, D. R. (2008). What I have learned so far: Observations on managing an academic accounting career. *Issues in Accounting Education, 23*(1), 53–66.

Hunt, S. C., Eaton, T. V., & Reinstein, A. (2009). Accounting faculty job search in a seller's market. *Issues in Accounting Education, 24*(2), 157–185.

Nathan, S., Hermanson, D. R., & Hermanson, R. H. (1998). Co-authoring in refereed journals: Views of accounting faculty and department chairs. *Issues in Accounting Education, 13*(1), 79–92.

Stone, D. N. (1996). Getting tenure in accounting: A personal account of learning to dance with the mountain. *Issues in Accounting Education, 11*(1), 187–201.

Walker, K. B., Fleischman, G. M., & Stephenson, T. (2010). The incidence of documented standards for research in departments of accounting at US institutions. *Journal of Accounting Education, 28*(2), 43–57.

APPENDIX A: APPROXIMATE TIMELINE

This appendix contains an approximate job market timeline with key dates indicated. Year t is defined as the year faculty employment begins.

Date	Task		Description
January$_{t-1}$	Submission deadline		Submission deadline for the AAA annual meeting for paper presentation.[a]
May$_{t-1}$	Plan development deadline		This should be viewed as the latest point candidates should have discussed with their advisor their timeline for graduation as well as their target market and how competitive they will be in their desired market.
June$_{t-1}$	Schedule AAA annual meeting interviews		If candidates choose to formally recruit at the AAA annual meeting, they can begin applying to selected jobs and setting up interviews. Candidates should be careful not to fill their schedules as schools will continue to post openings up until the meeting.
August$_{t-1}$	AAA annual meeting	Fall Recruiting Window	
Early fall$_{t-1}$	Defend proposal		This should be viewed as the latest reasonable time to have this completed to stay on track. The sooner this is completed, the more marketable the candidate becomes.
October$_{t-1}$	Rookie Camp registration deadline		
November$_{t-1}$			
December$_{t-1}$	Rookie Camp	Spring Recruiting Window	
Spring$_t$			Candidates should be aware that most universities require significant lead time in scheduling the dissertation defense, as well as requiring the defense to be completed well before the end of the semester and should plan accordingly.
April$_t$			
May/June$_t$	Graduation		
August/September$_t$	Start job		

[a]Presenting a paper at the AAA annual meeting is an opportunity for candidates to showcase their presentation skills and research capabilities; however, candidates should be aware that presenting *and* interviewing at the same conference will be time and energy consuming. We advise presenting only if the candidate is comfortable doing so, or if the candidate is required to for funding purposes.
Note: The "Fall Recruiting Window" period extends from August$_{t-1}$ through Nov$_{t-1}$, and the "Spring Recruiting Window" runs from Dec$_{t-1}$ through April$_t$.

APPENDIX B: COMMON JOB POSTING SOURCES

- American Accounting Association Career Center http://careercenter. aaahq.org
- Social Science Research Network (SSRN) http://www.ssrn.com/update/ arn/arnjob/arn_job.html
- *The Accounting Review* http://aaapubs.org/loi/accr
- HigherEdJobs https://www.higheredjobs.com/faculty/search.cfm?Job Cat=45

APPENDIX C: SAMPLE QUESTION GUIDE FOR CANDIDATES

Detailed Questions One Might Ask Faculty Members, Including the Chair

Research

1. What data feeds do accounting faculty have access to (e.g., WRDS, Compustat)?
2. Is there a conference travel budget, and if so how is it allocated?
3. Are there graduate assistants available for research and/or teaching support?
   a. Level of student (Ph.D., Macc, MBA, etc.) and number of hours?
4. Is there a budget for software needs (Stata, SAS, etc.)?
5. Does the department have a mentorship program (formal or informal)?
   a. Are senior faculty open to working with junior faculty? Are all mentors research active?
6. What are expectations for tenure?
   a. Is there a target journal list?
   b. What were the records of the most recently tenured and denied faculty members?
7. Is there summer research funding available?
8. Will I receive a (new) computer meeting my research needs?
   a. Are there startup funds available for my professional development?
9. Do you host regular research workshops here, or is there another university nearby that does?
10. How supportive is the Dean/Provost to this department/college?

Teaching

1. Specifically, which courses would I likely be assigned in this new position?
2. What is the "normal" number of sections and preps taught per year?
3. How long would I likely keep the schedule assigned?
4. Are there course releases available for research productivity?
5. What is the average class size?
6. What days and times of the week would I normally be teaching?
   a. Would I be required to teach on another campus?
7. Is summer teaching required or optional, and how is it assigned?
8. Are classrooms technologically advanced (Smart rooms)?
9. What are the student body demographics?

Service

1. What does a typical service assignment look like for both untenured and tenured faculty?
2. Would I be required to advise students? Formally?
3. Is there a budget for maintaining professional affiliations (AAA, CPA, AICPA, etc.)?

Other

1. What is the timeline for filling the position I am interviewing for?
2. Why is this position open/what has turnover looked like in recent years?
   a. Why have faculty left? May I have their names should I choose to contact them?
3. What is your favorite/least favorite thing about this department/college/ university/town?
   a. Adequate school quality for children, best areas of town to live, etc.
4. Have the expectations you had as a new hire been met?
5. What would you change about the department if you could?
6. What other benefits does the university offer?
   a. Retirement, health, tuition for family, moving allowance, gym access, etc.
7. How are raises typically structured for merit and/or promotion?
8. Are there resources available for finding employment for my spouse?
9. Let me explain why I think I would be a good fit here, beyond the geographic location ...

Questions One Might Ask Administrators, Such as the Dean

1. What is your vision for the college, and how does the department of accounting fit into that vision?
2. How would you describe the accounting department to a colleague?
3. What are the greatest strengths of the accounting department?
4. What are you looking for in hiring a new faculty member for the accounting department?

APPENDIX D: STRUCTURED INTERVIEW QUESTIONS

We asked the questions below to each of the participants in our structured interviews.

1. At what university did you earn your Ph.D.?
2. What is your job history since your Ph.D. was granted?
3. When you were in your Ph.D. program, would you have classified yourself as an international student?
4. What is your primary research methodology?
5. We are also interested in the following basic characteristics/resources of your current employer:
   a. What is the normal teaching load for your position?
   b. What is the normal number of preps for that load in a given year?
   c. What types of service requirements are you asked to perform?
   d. What data and/or experimental resources do you have access to for conducting research?
   e. Generally, what is your personal budget for research and professional development?
   f. Do you have access to other types of resources not listed and/or ones that may be unique to your institution?
6. Thinking about your search process for an academic position, did you have a strategy in terms of participating in a fall versus spring market?
   a. What "market" would you say you participated in?
   b. How did you view the AAA meeting in terms of job placement?
   c. Rookie Camp?
7. What do you think was the going amount of work-in-process that was expected by the potential employers in your market?
   a. Be specific on stages of projects and quality of target journals.

8. What was the best piece of advice you received for preparing for the job market?
9. Looking back, what do you wish you would have known?
10. Do you think a consolidated paper providing information about the critical aspects of the accounting academic job market would have been useful?
    a. Are there specific elements you think such a paper should contain?
11. Do you think you would have found a specific interview question set for candidates to be useful in formulating questions to ask as part of the interview process?
    a. Are there specific questions that you were glad you asked or wished you had asked?
12. Were there any surprises and/or unexpected events/questions/interactions during your own recruiting experience?
    a. How did you handle it?
    b. Would you handle it the same way again?
13. What common mistakes do you think job candidates make?
14. Is there anything else you would like to say about the accounting academic job market that you feel is important and hasn't been discussed here?

Printed in the USA/Agawam, MA
February 26, 2016

631284.025